T0381003

I'm
ON MY
Way

A MEMOIR OF FAITH, LOVE AND LAUGHTER

ALETHA J. SOLOMON

authorHOUSE

AuthorHouse™
1663 Liberty Drive
Bloomington, IN 47403
www.authorhouse.com
Phone: 833-262-8899

Published by AuthorHouse 03/08/2023

ISBN: 979-8-8230-0146-5 (sc)
ISBN: 979-8-8230-0145-8 (e)

Library of Congress Control Number: 2023903468

Print information available on the last page.

This book is printed on acid-free paper.

"The Lord makes firm the steps of the one who delights in him; though he may stumble, he will not fall, for the Lord upholds him with his hand.

Psalm 37:23-24 NIV

Contents

Part 12 Generational House

Dedication

I thank God for the wisdom, knowledge, and gifts needed to write this book.

This book is dedicated to my daughter Tai-Tanisha. Thanks for her counsel, support, kindness, love, and helpfulness. She is and has been the joy of my life. Every day I thank God for her. She makes me laugh, although sometimes we disagree. However, in the end, we love each other fully. There is nothing she would not do for me.

My daughter acquired the travel gene from my mom and me. She has been to more overseas destinations than I have. One day, I hope we revisit them together.

Hopefully, this book will bring smiles as she recalls these memories. I have captured many of the highlights. This book is an enduring collection of truths that will be passed down to her children and grandchildren forever.

Thank God for my daughter. She is my "SHERO."

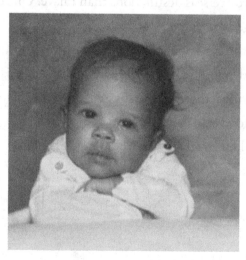

I LOVE YOU TAI-TANISHA

AMONG MY MANY BLESSINGS ARE MY FAMILY, L R BACKROW KRISTIA, MICHAEL II, TAI-TANISHA, MICHELLE, CARLOS, RAFAEL. L-R FRONTROW SKY, GAVEN, AVA'MARIE, KA'RINA, AND RAELYN. (NOT PICTURED MICHAEL AND AKEEM)

Preface

Aletha Solomon shares events from her earliest memory until today. She identifies with those who raised and taught her, leaving a lasting impression on her life. Life lessons have been shown to positively impact her life, and she wants to pass that concept along to others. She hopes you will permit this work to serve as a type of role model in your life. She was always encouraged to show selfless love for all and grasp everything she could learn from watching and listening to her role models.

In her life, she was motivated to seek and find those whom society may have crossed off: showing love to children who had no positive role models in their lives, primarily through mentoring and offering help, while volunteering and giving aid to seniors, and families.

When she began this book, it took time for her to see some elements of herself that she had never focused on before. She is typically soft-spoken and not argumentative. However, she is firm in decision-making and instructions, usually operating in a teaching mode. This has made inroads, opened doors, and created passion in her heart.

The book title suggests a road runner, who never stopped to smell the roses, but she did many times. In fact, her favorite flower is a yellow rose.

The journey will likely spark many of you to reach back and share memories that should be preserved while teaching life lessons for future generations to enjoy.

Introduction

Hopefully, you will read between the lines of these stories to feel like you were there. These are all true, and some are pretty funny. I can't stop laughing at myself and others as I read some of these shenanigans. You may see the humor encased in the narrative and laugh out loud too. My goal is to place each of my readers on the scene of the action; feel the essence and emotion of what was happening, as if you were there decades ago.

My unique lifestyle and career could not have been planned; it indeed was an act of God. I was always on the road. Work experience took me to places all over the country where I met people from all walks of life and have continued many of those relationships for years. Travel is the glue to most of these stories.

Life moments are captured on the page in different ways and from different points of view. My individual writing style allows for a story written in a child's voice and from their perspective in one chapter, and in a separate chapter, the adult speaks. The sequencing of the stories, not chronologically ordering them, is intentional. Here is a glimpse of how I see the world through technology, travel, fellowship, faith, and family.

This writing challenge gave me the look-back needed to pass precious memories to family and friends for generations to come. To confirm distances, years, and landmarks, I reached out to relatives to get their take on some of the details I may have forgotten (or chosen to forget, *whatever*). I did not exaggerate; it's all true. However, I only included uplifting stories. "If you can't say something good about someone, don't say anything at all" is my motto.

Please share this book with your children, public libraries, schools, churches, and anyone who might enjoy a good read and a hearty laugh.

PART 1

Lesson Learned

In their hearts humans plan their course, but the LORD establishes their steps.

Proverbs 16:9 NIV

Retired, Really?

$\mathcal{P}$ennsylvania would be my last transfer. My new location would involve much more traveling, technical design consulting, supervising, and customer education/training. This is where I first learned how much I enjoy working from home. Quite a bit of the system design work was done there, preparing for my next customer cutover. Hold up a minute; let me explain my work. My role as an AT&T manager was to design communication solutions for existing and new customers. I was a corporate consultant for telecommunications, data, computers, and networking.

Using the site's organization chart, department operations, employee job responsibilities, and manager coverage areas, I could design the new system to a tee from home and then travel to the site to implement the changeover. Getting to my site, setting up the training, and meeting with management before the employees arrived meant taking an extra early flight. I wouldn't say I liked the six a.m. flights every week, but I endured. This scenario went on for many years.

Coordinating corporate office system cutovers with their communications system and departmental work styles was often a pain. Many of the employees were resistant to changes they did not want. Initially, some would continue the work on scraps of paper rather than conform to the new software package designed and programmed specifically for their office. As soon as the office changed to the new system, employees found it more challenging to maintain the workload on slips of paper and other workarounds. Transitioning to the new system became the only way to accomplish the work that was needed.

My communications career ended in Pennsylvania with retirement and rest from jet lag. The last east coast team meeting meant flying into New York. Waking up on the plane, I noticed we were over the Verrazano Narrows Bridge, and knew La Guardia Airport was close. The iconic recognizable World Trade Center Towers were in view, and I knew we were about to land. This would be the last time I would see the World Trade Center Towers. Less than six weeks later, they were gone. After the bombing tragedy, I realized that only six weeks separated my flight, the World Trade Center planes, and the disaster. It could have been my plane. Thank God for favor.

Staying home and looking out of my front window at all the people going to work in the snow made me enjoy retirement all the more. I said, "too bad." Now I can stay up late and sleep in late. Remember, sleep is my best friend.

No work for me; "I'm done." That's almost true. No paid work for me. Volunteering as an IRS tax preparer has kept my interest for eight years here in Alabama. I enjoy it even if I do not get paid. I have learned that it is not always about the money that brings happiness. The feeling you get from giving what you have to someone in need can be the best, even when it's giving knowledge and preparing their tax return.

One of the churches here is excited about participating in Angel Tree Ministries for the first time. The ministry will bless children who have an incarcerated parent during the holidays. I have worked with that ministry in Pittsburgh and agreed to assist this church. They completed last Christmas season and are looking forward to this year. Before moving here, I found myself supporting volunteer Christian mentors for several years. Anything I can do to bring love and joy to children is good for me.

God has blessed me in my career, and now I can give to others allowing His light to shine through me by extending a helping hand where needed.

Alabama

Eight years ago, I got tired of making a two-day drive to visit my family for graduations, birthday celebrations, and holidays. I had already retired, and nothing was keeping me in Pennsylvania. I asked myself, "why not move there?" Not long afterward, I did.

When I first arrived, the small town seemed quaint and slow. I found a little larger town close by and moved there instead. I did not know anyone but my family. I found myself traveling locally to see my family and the few other people I had met. It was at least a half-hour drive one way to my daughter's house.

I met Gloria, Z.I., Lucile, and Judy when I got involved with tax preparation. Now I have four friends. I am still working with that crew. Don't get it twisted; it is work, but there is no pay. I like this volunteer gig. This is my way of giving back to the community and getting acclimated to southern lifestyles through conversations with clients.

Establishing myself at the chapel on Ft. Rucker Military Installation and volunteering in the nursery during worship service was quite rewarding. Deciding to move closer to the action, I had a house built in a new development, and now my travel to anywhere is usually ten minutes max, there are no freeways, no traffic jams, or morning or evening rush hours. We are talking about a small town, tiny.

My home is just the way I like it. Everyone that comes over hopefully will feel right at home too. I selected everything during the build, and it is perfect. Why did it take me so long to get here? The lesson is that you don't have to be in a crowded city with traffic to find fun and enjoy life. It's just the opposite; more fun, peace, and joy are found in a small-town environment where you can take your time as you enjoy doing everything. Don't forget "nothing before its time." I like it here, just far enough from everywhere and everybody.

It feels like home. What reminds me of home are all of my items that have special memories. Photographs that put a smile on my face just thinking about them, especially of the places I have lived and visited, feel like home. Actually, anything that conjures up warm feelings reminds me of home. Living in places in the North, Midwest, East, and South has shown me that God provides the warmth and family I need to feel right at home wherever I am. Having the most amazing friends, family, and people who care about me across the country, lets me know that home is a feeling, not a place. I pray that I replicate that feeling of home with anyone God places in my path and in my presence. There is an old saying I heard years ago, that home is wherever you hang your hat, I agree.

Oatmeal

Ring. Ring. That can not be the alarm. Just keep sleeping. Soon you will not hear it. (Drifting back to sleep.) I finally learned to ignore it so I wouldn't hear it. Staying up late was easy, but not so with getting up early when you are seven years old.

"Time to get up," I could hear my mom calling my name, "Letha, Letha, Letha Joyce, get out of that bed now." Then, "get up; I don't hear anything up there," she yelled. Turning over on my pillow and covering my head with the blanket did not stop her yelling. At that point, I said, "OK, I am up." (Of course, that was not true)

Soon I felt the cover yanked off me, "No, don't do that," I frowned. "You will not have time to eat breakfast if you do not get up right now," said mom. Finally, my feet hit the cool floor as I wiped the sleep from my eyes. I looked around and took a deep breath as I stretched and stood up straight, wondering what was for breakfast today.

When I first started school, the practice was to lay your clothes out at night, underwear, socks, outerwear, and accessories. That way, once I was finally up, getting everything on did not require much time.

Glancing at my clock, "oh, no," I only have until that long hand gets on the five before I need to leave for school. (I did not know how to tell time yet.) Running through the bathroom, throwing my clothes on, and brushing my hair, happened in record time. Running down the steps, out of breath, realizing I had not made my bed, I kept going. Of course, I would later hear about that. I still expected breakfast. Kids knew you did not go to school without breakfast. Our teacher told us it was the most important meal of the day. We needed it to learn.

At the bottom of the steps stood my mom with my coat stretched out in her hands, saying, "Put your arm in here," motioning to the coat sleeve. When my arms were in both sleeves, I was spun around to face my mom; she buttoned up my coat, hung my book bag on my shoulder, and pushed me out the door, closing and locking it behind me. I think I heard her say, "Have a good day."

Boom, the door was shut. I stood on the porch startled, with brows furred. What just happened? Did she forget that I had not had my breakfast? Remembering that there was no smell coming from the kitchen, I knocked on the locked door, no answer. Hurt, I slowly walked to the edge of the porch, looking back over my shoulder to see if the door had opened. It did not. Slowly going down the steps, tears began to well up in my eyes. Shuffling down the walkway, glancing back again, tears flooded down my cheeks. There were no kids on my route today. I continued to look down at the sidewalk the entire way to school, not wanting anyone to see me crying.

It took longer to get to school today; it seemed like I would never get there. My mind was traveling a hundred miles an hour, trying to get my arms around what happened, to no avail.

Arriving at school, no one was in the hallway. I must be late. No one would see me as I put my coat in my locker. Wiping my face and nose, I sniffled and went to my class. More tears started coming. I put my head on my desk. Soon the teacher came to check if I was all right. As soon as she looked at me, she asked, "Are you......," the flood waters erupted, and tears came from deep inside. My face was all screwed up as I tried to answer the question she never quite asked. Crying and talking at the same time were not working out very well. She could not understand what I was trying to say. Holding my arm, she helped me up and offered me a tissue as we walked to the office.

Sitting in the office while my teacher spoke to the "office lady." They asked me simultaneously, "What is the matter, baby?" Sniffling, crying, and getting just a few understandable words out, I announced in a crackling voice, "My mom would not give me any breakfast." Glancing at each other, the "office lady" says, "Honey, I'm sorry. If you are hungry, we can fix that." I said, "I am hungry." The teacher returned to her classroom and the "office lady" took me up the stairs near the office. Then up another set of stairs that I had never gone up before. Two large doors on the left opened into a vast room partially filled with students seated four at a table, eating. Staring around the room, I saw windows across the front and on both sides. The room was very bright.

None of these students looked familiar. I had never seen any of them in the hall, in classrooms, or after school. Who were they, and why were they up here eating breakfast? Years later, I found out that was called the open-air classroom for students with asthma and other concerns. The rest of us never got to enjoy breakfast at school. This was before there was any eating at school, breakfast, or lunch (We all walked home for lunch). They sat me at a small table, alone. Someone brought me oatmeal with brown sugar and milk. They put orange juice on the table and a container of regular milk.

Tasting the oatmeal after stirring it up made me smile for the first time today, ahh, breakfast. It was warm and soothing. I looked around as I slowly ate and noticed the other kids looking back at me. The "office lady" had dropped me off, and someone else took me back to the office when I was done. Happily, I skipped down the steps since my stomach was full, and there were no more tears. I have no memories of earlier in the day when I was put out of the house, hungry. When the office door opened and we went in, my eyes got big, my heart stopped, and it was hard to breathe. Who was sitting there but my Mother? What? Why was she here? Oh my gosh, I was scared now. The "office lady" came and seated us in her office. She explained the earlier events of my day at school while explaining the importance of breakfast and the connection between nutrition and learning. Mom was agreeable and said she understood. When the "office lady" was done, she let my mom go and sent me back to class. We walked halfway down the hall together, and mom said, "Have a good day; I'll see you when you get home." I went to my class, and mom went down the stairs and left the school.

The rest of the day caught me wondering if my mom would kill me when I got home. I thought I was going to die. School is over, and I'm headed home. Suddenly, tears began to well up in my eyes as I slowly started walking. (I didn't want to get home too fast to die). The closer I got to my house, the slower I walked. My heart began to beat faster as the tears flowed.

Ok, I'm at my house. I walked up the stairs and knocked on the door, which opened immediately. Mom said, "Hi, how was your day?" My eyes were questioning why I was not dead yet. I said, "It was fine." Immediately I went up to my room.

To this day, it has never been spoken of again. The lesson taught me that coming downstairs late gets you no breakfast and was reinforced by the "office lady" calling mom to the school while I thought I had gotten over.

It took all that both lessons had to offer to teach me several life lessons: (1) always allow yourself enough time, (2) do not think you are going to die when you were never spanked or abused before, (3) and a mother's true love.

Toilet Water

Most of you are probably not old enough to remember "toilet water." It was a type of lady's perfume. I believe under the brand name *Evening in Paris*. I saw this bottle on the shelf in the bathroom every day. Something told me to take the initiative to handle the toilet water so no one else would have to do it. I could handle this. The bottle that held the toilet water was a darker blue color; you couldn't see inside without opening the top. The scent was lovely. The toilet bowl did not seem to be the place to put this beautiful fragrance. I thought it must go in the back tank that held the fresh water.

Opening the tank by taking the lid off, I unsecured the top of the bottle that held the toilet water and put two drops into the tank. I put the lid back on the toilet, closed the bottle, and put it away for the next day. Each day I would repeat this chore. I was convinced that this toilet water did something special for the toilet, and indeed my family would be pleased that I did this without even being asked.

One day when the bottle was empty, I asked if someone could buy some more because I had used all of it. They asked, "what did I mean?" I explained how I had taken care of the toilet by putting the toilet water in daily. They looked at each other, then back at me, and then back to each other before laughing their heads off. They carefully explained to me that this was a perfume for women not for the toilet. It should not have been wasted putting it in the toilet. The lesson learned is that I should have asked before using something that did not belong to me.

Puppy Painting

Our neighborhood was safe. No one was breaking in or kidnapping kids in my neighborhood, at least I never knew of any. That doesn't mean a three-year-old has the freedom to move around the neighborhood doing whatever she wants, does it? Let's see if it does.

Who was your best friend at three years old? Grandma was my best friend. My mom worked, so grandma took care of me during the day. I was not old enough to go to school yet. We ate together during the day, and she combed and brushed my hair when she wanted me to nap. It put me to sleep every time. We took walks to the store and usually sat on the porch while she cooked.

Grandma felt she knew me well enough that she could take her eyes off me for one moment and I would be ok. I was a child you could trust. After all, I was three years old. She knew me so well that she could predict my every move. Get in trouble, not me, because there were no other children for me to get in trouble with. How could I get in trouble? When we were not watching Soap Operas or Soupy Sales on TV, we sat on the porch glider, slowly swinging. Sometimes we sang while watching people and cars. I had a cute doll, and it was always with me. We had a dog named King. He was quiet and sat near the glider. It was grandma and me, "BFFs."

Grandma was the main cook during those years, and mom and auntie went to work during the day. There was always something in the oven. Occasionally, she would check the food to ensure it didn't burn. When the phone rang, she had to run and grab it since no one had yet to create cell phones, cordless phones, voicemails, or caller ID. You either got it, or you missed it. "Shucks," she would say when that happened.

I heard the phone ringing and said, "grandma, the phone is ringing." She jumped up and ran to get it. While she was in the house, I could hear her laughing and talking as I sat swinging on the porch glider. She was gone a long time. I decided to get up from the glider and sit on the steps, which was ok. I often would sit on the steps, and I liked it. She kept a sharp eye on me, watching from inside the house.

I heard some puppies yipping a couple of houses down, and I looked back to see if I could ask grandma if we could go and see them, but I could not see her. Slipping off the porch, I went to see the puppies, planning to return before grandma missed me. The puppies were only two houses down. Some men on ladders were painting that house earlier, but I did not see them. Maybe they had gone for lunch; I don't know. The puppies were in a box near the porch. They were so cute, all six of them. I looked around to see who was there. All I wanted to do was touch them and maybe pick them up. They each wanted me to get them as they tried to climb out to get to me. I loved them. Picking them up and rubbing them was so much fun; I even kissed one.

Next to the box of puppies was some paint that the men used to paint the house before they left. I am not sure what color the paint was, but my mom told me years later that it was a pastel color. One by one, I dipped the puppies completely in the buckets of paint and put each one back in the box. They shook and tried to open their eyes. They were so cute. I noticed that something was wrong. They were not playful anymore; they just lay there. The paint was all over me and my clothes. I tried to wipe the paint off my hands, rubbing them on my shirt and pants. That made it worst. Soon, Mrs. Honeybuss came out on the porch because she heard some noise from the puppies. It was a screeching sound, not barking. I guess it sounded like something or someone was getting them.

As she came out onto her porch, she was startled: eyes wide open, mouth as well, and hands up in the air. She could hardly speak. Suddenly she yelled, "Mitch, guys, come quick." She turned to run and call my grandma on her phone. "Emma, your granddaughter has walked down to my house. She is ok, but I think you better come and see this," she said, as she hung up the phone. "You, little girl, sit here on the steps. Your grandma is coming to get you. What were you doing to the puppies? Why did you put them in the paint?" Guys, see if you can wipe off the puppies, and I will call the vet to see what to do," said Mrs. Honeybuss.

Grandma came running down the street with her slippers on her feet. She was glad I was all right, even though she didn't know I had left the porch. Grandma appeared breathless when she arrived. "First, I went to answer the phone. When I got off the phone, I checked the food in the oven. It must have taken longer than I thought. Usually, she would sit still on the glider, and there was never any problem, but not today," grandma said. It was as though the puppies called me, and I was mesmerized to go and see them. The guys tried to wipe the puppies, but the thick paint would not come off their fur. The paint remover was too harsh on the puppies' skin. The puppies' eyes were still shut. They couldn't even see how sad I was that the paint was not good for them.

The puppy doctor asked them to bring the puppies to his office. Someone grabbed the box of puppies, put them in the car, and drove off. Still sitting on the steps, I was confused about what was happening. Mrs. Honeybuss and grandma explained, "the paint was cute on the puppies, but it would probably make them sick. That's why they had to go to the doctor." Maybe the doctor could get the paint off of them. They knew I was trying to make them beautiful, but I should have asked before leaving the porch and touching the puppies. Both of them started laughing and saying, "Oh lordy, lordy," as grandma and I walked back home.

When my mom and everybody else came home, the story was told about the day's happenings. (In fact, this annual story kept being told and retold.) Everyone laughed and just shook their heads as they looked at me. I did not get in trouble; maybe I should have. Of course not; no, I should not have. Maybe grandma should have gotten in trouble for leaving me alone for such a long time, laughing and talking on the phone, and then checking for burnt food in the oven. Who knows, maybe she got a time-out. Whatever you do, I beg you, don't breathe a word of this to her; she was my favorite. It would break her heart all the way up in heaven.

Later, we found that the puppies did okay for a few weeks but did not make it, which again made me sad. I said, "I will never paint puppies ever again." To this day, I never did. The lesson is never to leave your three-year-old near puppies and a pail of paint. You would be surprised what could possibly happen.

Authors Note:

In all seriousness, as much as this story is a part of my family history, I do not condone animal cruelty or any action causing harm to animals. I believe in loving all of God's creatures.

Communication

At particular times during the year, especially at Christmas, family members would schedule an appointment, get all fancy and go to a photo studio to get professional photographs taken to stick inside their Christmas cards or to hand out. Someone always had a "Brownie" camera often only used to capture special moments. When the roll of film in the camera was complete, you had to remove the roll and drop the film off at the drug store to be developed and printed. You will be given a pickup date when the pictures would be ready, so you can come in, pay, and pick them up. The first time you see the images might be weeks or months from when you took them.

Payphones were on every corner, in every store and terminal. You could make a local call within the city limits for a nickel. Later the local calls went to a dime. An operator was necessary to make a long-distance call, and the cost was determined by the distance of the call and how long you talked. The operator would tell you how much to put in before they connected your call. When your time was up, the operator would break into your call and tell you how much more to put in if you plan to continue the conversation, or they would cancel your call.

Working for the telephone company, I always had the latest communication devices. When I started work, mobile car and cell phones appeared as far-off inventions. However, a few decades later, they were the hot rave. In the beginning, only a few people had them or wanted them. There were stories of getting radiation in your head, and that cell phones would cause cancer if you used them. The rays that carried the call through the air would pass through your body, even though you can't see them, or they could harm you in other ways. Many fables were out there, and the public was slow to determine what to believe.

My company gave managers, and a few other employees pagers, otherwise known as beepers. They were small and would fit in the palm of your hand. You clipped the beeper onto your waistband or purse strap. It was not like a phone; you could not answer or talk on it. The beeper had a regular number, and it would beep when anyone dialed your number. The caller's number showed on the tiny screen. When you are ready to contact the person trying to reach you, dial the number displayed on the beepers screen from a regular phone.

Too often, when I was on the freeway entrance ramp, my beeper would go off. I had to take the next exit and find a payphone to return the page. That exercise would sometimes happen several times a day. I can tell you where every payphone was located in any city I worked in. You never left the office without a handful of dimes to feed the payphones during your day. Later, managers were given a mobile car phone. I no longer had to stop at every payphone, rain or shine, to return a page.

Today there are no payphones on corners or in public places, no mobile or car phones, and no operators are needed to connect and charge calls, local or long distance. It's been a while since I have seen a payphone. Mobile car phones had a short life because cell phones removed the need for them. People have gotten over the myths about the dangers of cell phones causing cancer. Almost everyone has a cell phone, even children. You will find multiple cell phones in most homes, each with a different number. The younger generations are not opting to have house phones anymore.

Phones

Most people rely solely on their cell phones. Cell phones allow people to be more accessible because they are with them at all times, in the house, car, work, and other places. When the cell phone became popular, most people disconnected their house phones, saving them money while making themselves more available. You could be reached 24/7 on your cell phone because it was in your pocket or purse. The house phone could only be accessed at home.

As the demand for cell phones grew, manufacturers began to incorporate more and more technology while making the phones smaller and smaller. You now could hold the phone in the palm of your hand or carry it in your pocket. These phones with added technology are known as smartphones. Conference calls and video calls can be made by everyone with a smartphone. Phones, from their inception, allowed you to talk and hear the person you were talking to but not to see them. With smartphone technology and picture phones in conference rooms, you also can see who you are talking to. You can make more than one call at a time. You can call long distance without the aid of an operator, and send and receive mail without a mail carrier, envelope, stamp, or post office. Photos are snapped, viewed, and shared without rolls of film having to be developed and printed, plus no drop-off and pickup sites were involved.

The "smartphone," is a cell phone with call capabilities plus internet service. In 1989 the world wide web was founded, allowing the rapid speed of data and information across networks globally. We commonly refer to this service as the internet. Most cell phone users today do more than make and receive calls on their phones. These phones can do so many things that they are referred to as smartphones. The internet through your phone will let you: read, watch television and movies, mail, make appointments, alarm clocks, and many other services. There is nothing like a smartphone. With a tiny device that fits in the palm of your hand and weighs almost nothing, you don't have to have a house phone, computer, television, radio, record player, stereo, or car phone. If that was not enough to get your head spinning, now we have the "smart car." I have one, which is undoubtedly smarter than I am, but I am catching up.

The uniqueness of this type of phone was that you could call from anywhere. You did not have to be attached to a cord in your hallway or at home. Everything is so instant now.

In the late 1980s, when I was given a car phone for my work vehicle, I could only call what they now refer to as "landlines" or co-workers who had the same job I did and who also were given a car phone. No ordinary people had car or cell phones yet. Later, a few people had bag phones. It was just that, a phone in a leather bag twice the size of a brick and equally heavy. By 1990, cell phones had gained popularity. Still, not many people were able to afford them. Most young people wanted them. My age group was still trying to decide on the risk of "cellular waves" harming your body. For the most part, all you did on this new device was make and receive calls. By the late 1990s, going into the new millennium, everybody wanted one, even children.

Our "easy lives" have caused us to devalue and have less deeply rooted relationships. We do not have the depth of friendships once held. Many of our young people can't look each other eye to eye while speaking because they are most often communicating on a device held in their hand. Too many children/people are abused over the network. Too many others find ways to do hateful things and make unhealthy images available for all to see. Young people don't spell or read as well as they should because they "text" each other in abbreviations, slang, symbols, and icons. Basic math is done on a calculator application on the cell phone, taking the easy way out. Texting and emailing from your cell phone has removed the joy of receiving a letter in the mail and sitting down and reading each word.

For those immersed in social media, your daily feelings, activities, thoughts, and plans can be shared over the network, i.e., Facebook. Whether or not you want feedback, you will get comments and opinions that could sway your life's direction from people you barely call acquaintances. I don't wish to hear everything a person does and certainly don't want them to hear or comment on everything I do. If I comment on someones posting and another of their friends responds to my comment in an unpleasant way, this could start a "text" war with someone I don't know. My photographs are not to be shared on Instagram with strangers, and I don't want to see theirs. When a topic is on Twitter, anyone can jump in to give their thoughts and opinions. They don't even have to be on a "friend list." Everybody can respond to everybody else; it gets crazy.

The sad thing is that few on Facebook, Instagram, Twitter, or other social media outlets have any personal connection or care deeply about the issues, statuses, and pictures submitted through the various outlets. I want to be deeply connected to those I call "friends." To have hundreds or thousands of friends, as some people do, is absurd. There is no way you can be personally or genuinely sincere about the feelings, issues, and concerns of that many people. It's superficial. These are not even close acquaintances. Once you comment on your page, it's out there, and you can't get it back.

Growing up, I believed that throughout your life, the average person had no more than a handful of friends and a few more acquaintances, and the rest just faces in a crowd. The good news is that the cell phone is a beautiful addition to our lifestyle. However, I don't want it to be a ball and chain that anyone can call me at any given moment and expect me to be instantly willing to answer their call on the first ring. Sometimes I choose not to answer and intentionally let the call go to voicemail, because I am not feeling "it." Thank goodness for caller ID. You can be sure that I will not return a call to an unrecognizable number that chooses not to leave a message. I refuse to be that accessible on this planet.

The lesson learned is that I want to go to a restaurant and notice people talking and laughing with those at their table, not doing something on their phones. Looking at the person you are talking to would be novel. Sooner than later, they will all suffer from "Text Neck."

I Am not Thankful...

Communication today is a very different animal than that of the past decades. The world we live in has gone from virtually two cans and a string just a few decades ago to an obsessive amount of differing types of communication technologies today.

The house phone was in the hallway at our house, with a cord permanently attached to the phone on one end and the wall on the other. It was the only phone in the house, with no privacy and in clear view of everybody. The calls were sometimes with people we didn't talk to daily. You didn't call the same person two, three, or four times a day. Calls were "as needed" rather than today's all-the-time, ball and chain calls. Months could pass between calls to family and friends who lived out of town and sometimes between those who lived in the same city.

For out-of-town calls, you needed an operator to connect you to the number you wanted, a single number or multiple numbers, known today as conference calls.

These calls were billed by the minute and could get pricey. You were genuinely glad to hear from them and were equally happy to stop what you were involved in and give that caller your undivided attention. We always had a chair right next to the phone. You might hear whoever answered the call say, "it's Uncle Willie." Everybody in the house would gather near that phone to listen to one side of the call because speakerphones had not been invented.

Something else, you looked forward to the mailman coming. Getting a letter from a friend or family member, local or long distance, was special. First, after getting the envelope in your hand, you sat down, opened your letter, and read it slowly, savoring every word that was written, audibly showing how much you enjoyed it. After dinner family was excited to hear you read the letter to them if it wasn't too personal. When was the last time you received a handwritten letter?

Downtown

My friend Carolyn, her brother Calvin and I asked to see a movie in a downtown theatre about three and a half miles away. We left with money for the bus to get there, money for the theatre, and money for some popcorn. We also made sure we had enough money to take the bus back. During those days, fast food chains did not exist on every corner. McDonald's and those kinds of restaurants were not in existence. There were only two different hamburger joints in three locations in the entire city. We always said one day we would stop at the one we passed while on the bus going downtown. Neither of us had ever been to a place where you could eat out like this. This was something new. Boy were we excited.

When the movie was over, we put our heads together and decided to walk back home, and use the bus money to stop at the hamburger place and buy a hamburger. We couldn't wait to get there.

This restaurant was about a quarter of the way home. We began our walk and finally reached the restaurant. We went in, looked at the menu on the wall, counted our money, and placed our order. They bagged up our items, and we continued our walk home, eating as we went. Those had to be the best hamburgers we ever had. Eating out did not exist back then. Our mothers made our hamburgers. After eating our hamburgers, we still had quite a distance before reaching home. We trudged along, "how much further" we kept asking ourselves. We knew we were not lost because we kept seeing familiar sights. Several buses passed us up going our way, but we had spent our bus money.

We continued our walk even though our legs were about to give out. We finally saw the turn-off for home. I could see the back of my house and couldn't get there fast enough. The hamburger was good, but I don't think it was good enough for a walk of that distance. The lesson learned is never to spend your bus money on something you did not have to have. Never, again.

PART 2

Church

He has shown you, O mortal, what is good. And what does the Lord require of you? To act justly and to love mercy and to walk humbly with your God.

Micah 6:8 NIV

Koinonia

Life is sometimes hard, do you agree? Work, kids, friends, family, and church can sometimes take the steam out of your stride. Being an overachiever doesn't help. I do not have ADHD, but sometimes it's as though I just finished an energy drink as I move to accomplish a task. Things seem to be going at warp speed. I try to finish everything on my to-do list, so I don't have to move them over to the next day's tasks. There is enough there already.

Don't get me wrong, I loved my work, especially since 90% required travel and out-of-town assignments. Also, I love going to church, and the worship music was always rich. The church occasionally found ways to use my time doing stuff other than worshipping. Some things that weren't getting completed did not require me to do them. I have learned that I did not have to bring closure to other people's assignments just because I thought they needed help. "No," didn't come out of my mouth enough. I firmly believe God places a calling on our lives and doesn't give us more than we can handle. Taking on responsibilities God did not give us creates stress when it could be avoided. It was my fault some of those things wound up on my plate. At some point, I would scream and say, "I have had enough; it's time for Koinonia."

At first, no one knew what that meant, but biblically speaking, it is the Greek word for fellowship. An email would go out to a select few who were also in much need of fellowship. Bobbi, Sheila, and Leonora were our regular Pittsburgh group, and occasionally one or two others were invited. The response was always, "where and how soon?" If you had asked any of us how we felt, we would have said we were just "ducky." That meant we each had lots of stuff from our work and other connections we wanted to not think about or bring to mind. It was as if we could put our heads underwater and our butts in the air and think only about good times and each other. Sometimes we had to remind each other to just be a duck when we were up to our necks with the pressures of life, work, and family. You know how ducks are; they simply let the water roll off their backs, with no concerns.

Koinonia, now this is an occasion you put on your calendar, and we let nothing or nobody compromise this time. We would meet and spend hours at dinner, not just eating but pouring out our hearts and sharing things that couldn't be shared with just anyone. No, I heard your thought; it was not gossip. We were all in the same boat, overworked in our jobs and sometimes overworked in the church.

Good Friday service was always a time of reflection and thankfulness for Christ's sacrifice for each of us. Most years, our conference of churches selected one site for all of its local churches to celebrate Good Friday together in one place. Since the sisterhood did not all attend the same church in our conference, the Good Friday service was a good time for us to get together, worship, and spend time afterward. A tradition was established years ago for us to leave the worship service together, dine, and catch up with each other's lives.

This time was exceptional; we all looked forward to sharing and loving each other. It allowed us to exhale and breathe deeply, letting out the issues of our day-to-day lives. Some of us have moved away, some have gone to glory, and others are not attending service anymore. Bobbi and I have shared how deeply we miss this time together, and nothing will be able to fill the missing place in our hearts. However, we can look back on those beautiful times with a smile and remember how God had blessed that time in the sisterhood.

Communion

My oldest grandson was always sticking to me like glue. Some say he was the favorite, but I do not have any favorites. However, he was allowed to come with me on a visit to Detroit. I grew up attending church, joining and faithfully serving wherever I lived.

In the Lutheran Church, children only participate in communion services after they reach a certain age and have completed training and have been confirmed. My grandchildren have all accepted Jesus and are baptized but had never had communion. In Detroit, we attended a service where communion was celebrated that Sunday. Knowing the heart and belief of my grandson, he was allowed to receive communion.

I told him we were having communion and explained what would happen during the service. However, I should have shared that their service served wine, not grape juice. Not wanting him to think more about the wine before taking communion, I left that part out. Knowing my grandson, I knew it would be better to have that conversation after service. There would be lots of questions.

After we received the communion, back at our pew, he kept nudging me and calling me "grandma," I chose not to look at him or answer. Soon I whispered, "not now. We will talk later." He was ok with that.

On the ride home, we discussed the celebration of wine and bread in communion, and he told me he understood. Of course, he was ready to tell my daughter that grandma had given him some wine. No problem that he threw me under the bus. She also grew up in church, and she understood.

Somehow I always have to crawl out from under that bus. After returning from Italy, where cheese pizza is called Margarita, the youngest grandson told his mom that grandma gave him a "margarita." It's the first and the last ones I have to worry about. I love them both.

Leonora

We were always members of Lutheran Churches in whatever city we lived in. After moving to Pennsylvania, my family and I began looking for a church to join. My co-worker, Bobbi, invited me to the church's special presentation about Christ Quanza. I enjoyed the presentation and decided to attend the weekly bible study. After feeling comfortable with the bible study, we came for the worship service one Sunday morning. The AMEZ Church was unfamiliar to me, but we were willing to get our feet wet in this denomination. The people were warm, and the sermons were just what we needed to hear.

Being inquisitive and wanting to know everything about what I involved myself in, I had many questions. God gave me a sister-friend named Leonora to help answer some of my questions. She spent time at the church teaching me everything about the African Methodist Episcopal Zion Church. Whenever I was not traveling for my job, she took me to conferences in town, out of town, and across town.

This was the perfect person for me to glean all I needed to know about the church and its beliefs and operational order. She was involved in every aspect of the church. It was as if she was "the lady who owned the church." As a trustee, she prepared detailed reports and coordinated events in every department at our church and conference. Many other hats were worn by her as well.

Leonora was an expert at being the church treasurer and keeping finite records down to the penny. One evening she invited my mom and me out for a bite to eat. Afterward, she wanted to stop at an electronics superstore. We were free for the evening and agreed. Little did I know it was a setup. She had plans to look at and ultimately purchase a desktop computer. Leonora said, "would you help me select a computer?" "Sure," I said. Never did I think about how this decision would change my life. We went in and looked at different models and options. Mentioning some of the standard features showed me that she had never used a computer; this was her first one. She asked if I would teach her how to use the computer if she purchased one. Of course, I would.

The computer went home with us in the back seat of her car. Unloading the boxes from the car, we set the computer up and powered it on. Only then did I realize she was telling the "whole" truth about her lack of computer skills. She even had to learn how to power it up. Oh, my work was cut out for me. She laid out the handwritten spreadsheets that covered virtually the entire rug, with information that would need to go into the computer. These spreadsheets spanned many years of the church's financial data. The objective was to build a program for current and future processes, not to input old reports. Evaluating this project, we came up with a good outline; however, it had to be modified repeatedly. I don't remember how many times.

First, she had to learn computer basics as I worked on developing a program to enter the handwritten data. Included in the transactions were various departments, ministries, and incoming and outgoing financial information for both the church and the parsonage. I developed formulas to combine the quarterly reports to create the annual report and eliminate redundancies. It was monumental, but it was not stressful since my student was very congenial, patient, and a quick learner. She was like my sister.

Occasionally, we needed to call Glenn, a friend, and neighbor who was our tech expert, to bail us out of a computer hardware issue. He responded quickly and explained things in a way we could grasp and move forward. If a second issue arose, Glenn would come immediately to resolve anything tech related without a complaint.

God was with us nightly as we plodded along, sometimes into the middle of the night, seeing small bites of success along the way. It took months of hard work for my student to become comfortable with technology. She followed instructions well, as she took notes in old-school shorthand. Remembering how she seldom throws anything away, she probably still has her dubious notes, today.

For many years we provided detailed reports with perfect accuracy thanks to Leonora. I will have to ask her if she still has those instructions in her notebook.

High Tea

While Leonora and I worked on learning the computer, the Missionary Department was busy planning for its first High Tea. Some friends flew in to support this function from Detroit, Washington D.C., Atlanta, and Denver. Of course, the flights came in at different times, much less on the same day. I went to the airport over and over to pick up guests who were flying in for the tea. Church hats are virtually a thing of the past. Years ago, women came to church "decked out," as we used to say. Most of the hats were big and had a veil in front of their eyes. Each woman seemed to try to outdo others with their ornate hats. They were looking good from head to toe. Almost no one wears church hats any longer. One of the requirements for the High Tea was to step back in time and bring out those beautiful hats and gloves at least one more time.

The arriving passengers were told (actually threatened) that they had better be able to show their hats when picked up at the airport, or they would be going back home to get one. God is good all the time. They all had a hat, even if it was under duress. My cousin Ida fussed the most. Proclaiming harshly that she did not want to wear that hat. She repeatedly asked, "do I really have to wear it?" Assuring me that it was going in the closet as soon as she got home and would never be seen again.

The afternoon High Tea was a success. The weather was grand, the hall was immaculately decorated, and the tables were dressed perfectly. The linen napkins, table clothes, silver flatware, tiered sandwich stands, tea cups, and teapots were divine. The presenters were excellent, and the pastors of the local churches were our servers. Everyone looked amazing, and each hat was a story in and of itself, some quite flamboyant.

The theme centered around Servant/Leadership. Each pastor was assigned a table of eight to serve. They did a fantastic job and looked suave and debonaire in their dark suits, bow ties, and cummerbunds. They were not only serving and entertaining their table but were entertained by those at the table. All I saw were smiles, and I heard plenty of laughter. They had fun teaching us how leaders can serve, and it was done to perfection. There could not have been a better lesson in a classroom.

Rev. R. Russell, my table server and pastor, gave the Invocation before the tea service began. Knowing him, you could surely count on laughs and a good time. He fit the occasion perfectly. He was the perfect example of servant leadership, as were all the other pastors. All the pastors enjoyed that day's laughs, fun, and fellowship.

Food was served in courses. Course I was a variety of sandwiches, Course II was Scones and Breads with different spreads and jams, and Course III was Petit Fours and Sweets. Several flavors of teas were available. There were musical selections, poetry reading, and a meditation during the meal. Everyone had a grand time.

When God brings people into my life, it blesses me. No matter what state I am living in, they will come, and I know it blesses them, also. In coming to the tea, friends from each state are now friends with one another because of the connection made by the power of God. Otherwise, they would probably not have met. Some call it Destiny or a God-predestined event. The sisterhood is unstoppable. Indeed they all traveled home with a smile on their faces and their tea hat in a bag. I can almost guarantee that none of their hats have been worn since then.

Love you all, Sheila, Tai-Tanisha, Marsha, Bobbi, Emily, Leonora, Lois, Ida, Viola, Mom, and Gwen. I am looking forward to getting together again soon.

Worlds Fair

The Worlds Fair came to New York. My church youth group, the Walther League, earned a chance to attend the fair. Surely I thought we would go on an airplane, but that did not happen. However, this was the best thing ever, and our parents turned us over to the youth leaders. We had a blast.

From Detroit, It took two days to travel there by van and by way of the Pennsylvania Turnpike. This was new, being able to stop for bathroom breaks and treats along the way. We got to go inside and get what we wanted. As a small child, my family traveled back and forth to my uncles between Michigan and Pennsylvania. I remember the word Turnpike but had never been able to get out and get food while traveling. Usually, they traveled overnight, and all of us children would be asleep.

I counted the license plates from different states, imagining my jigsaw puzzle of the U.S. map. I saw cars from states I had only seen on the map. Who were those people driving those cars? I bet they are all going to the fair, too.

There was a church in Pittsburgh whose youth group was expecting us. That was about at our halfway point to New York. They made dinner for us and prepared comfortable sleeping arrangements for the night. There was not much sleeping done. We played games, ate and talked about many things. We stayed up late, and breakfast was ready for us in the morning before we left to continue on our New York trip.

We had been invited to stay at different Lutheran Church parsonages in New York. After arriving, we saw huge buildings with many stories and hundreds of families living in each one. Traffic and taxi cabs were everywhere. It was so hot in New York that our clothes were sticking to us. No air moved; it was as still as a picture. People rushed around, going who knows where on foot, bikes, and cars. Sidewalk shopping was everywhere. Vendors sold clothes, vegetables, fruit, and miscellaneous items. Ladies pulled metal buggies with two wheels with what could be groceries and other purchased items. Kids were playing, skipping, and running. Babies were crying. Wow, what a great conglomerate of events. We saw lots of things I had never even imagined. Everyone was in a hurry to go where?

As a child in Michigan, you always looked forward with great anticipation to the start of the State Fair in September. There were vendors, animals, baked goods, all types of food for sale, amusement rides, hay rides, and pony rides. There were tons of people and lines everywhere. However, nothing about it prepared me for the New York Worlds Fair.

Soon after arriving at the Worlds Fair, I saw lines like I never saw before. Most of the people spoke in languages I had never heard. Some were dressed in their native attire and carried their babies in a weird way. Everybody was happy and treated each other in a loving way; even when we did not understand their language, it was fun.

We stayed in New York for several days and had an opportunity to see other sights. I was astounded at the number of people everywhere we went, not just at the fair but everywhere in New York. The buildings were so tall that you could barely see the sky unless you looked straight up.

You could buy franks, what we call dirty hot dogs, from a street corner vendor. They were the best hot dogs ever. We all wanted one every day. Pizza shops were all over as well. You didn't have to buy a whole pizza. I wasn't sure if they sold whole pizzas. It was sold by the slice, on the corners, in the subway stations, and everywhere you looked. You got your slice or your dirty frank and kept walking and eating. There was no sitting down at tables. This was truly fast food on the go. Everything about New York was amazing. I decided then that that's where I wanted to go when I became an adult. Believe it, that's what I did. It's the city that's so nice they had to name it twice, New York, New York.

Tabernacle

Church services today are different from those when I was a young child. I remember attending Tabernacle Baptist Church with my grandparents, where ladies dressed in fancy hats, gloves, fur stoles, and high heel shoes with stockings that had a seam up the back. Men usually wore three-piece suits, no matter how high the temperature was. All wore dress hats, and in chilly weather, all had overcoats.

I remember the men sitting in a separate section of the church. The ladies and children sat together. When I said sat, we sat very still and did not move or say anything. You did not ask any questions, and you better not have to go to the bathroom. You were asked to go before you went to church, and hopefully, you did. Anytime we went to service there, I never saw the bathroom. Was there one? Beats me, I couldn't tell you.

The people on your pew were squashed tightly together. It was virtually impossible to move even if you wanted to. Turning to the left, I was next to a lady wearing a fur stole with an animal head with eyes and teeth and paws with claws. The stole was over the woman's shoulder, and the animal's head, teeth, and claws were just at the level of a child's face, my face. I dared not look left. My mom, grandma, or aunt was on my other side. My aunt had one of these stoles, and I hoped that either my mom or grandma was next to me on my other side. The last thing I wanted was one of these scary dead animals on both sides of me.

While the talking was going on (sermon), it seemed like forever. I would try to sneak a half-head turn to get a glimpse at that animal. I quickly looked and turned away. It was so scary. The perfume the women wore was awful. I tried holding my breath so I could not breathe it in. After holding my breath for as long as possible, I had to breathe again. Between the animal on the stole, the awful perfume, and the tight seating, I could not wait for church to be over. One thing you did not do was complain. You, as they say, "grin and bear it." Church couldn't end quick enough for me.

Thank goodness that weird church dress code ended. I don't know when but I am glad it's gone. If there were scary animals and tight seating with awful perfume now, I believe the pastor might be the only one there, or maybe the men would still be sitting in their separate areas. Perhaps that's why they sat over there; they were probably scared to look at those animals and smell that awful perfume too.

Confirmation

In my early teens, the time had come for me to begin confirmation classes at the Lutheran Church. The classes were on Saturdays and lasted two years, meeting weekly. The confirmation class prepared you to go deeper in the study of the Bible and understand your church, and commit to Christ in your life.

Gilda, Cheryl, and I walked to the church each week. It was a long walk, but we made it. On the way to church, we passed a corner store that sold everything we wanted. There were dill pickles in a large jar, cookies three for a penny, and pieces of candy, two or three for a penny. We could go with a dime and leave with a bag full of goodies. We always attended class and stopped at the store. The one we looked forward to the most each week is unclear.

Taking the class entailed homework, and I would search the Bible extensively. I wanted to know everything and memorized much of what we had learned. I had some favorite stories and some favorite disciples.

One of the things I grew to like was our Friday evening youth meetings, the Walther League. We met every week. One Friday, we had an outing, and the following week we stayed in, had a lesson, and played a game indoors. We repeated this schedule and were never home on Friday nights. We loved hanging out, in addition to learning a lot. My faith walk was established significantly, and I am grateful for those Fridays in my youth.

PART 3

Moving/Traveling

But he said to me, "My grace is sufficient for you, for my power is made perfect in weakness." Therefore I will boast all the more gladly about my weaknesses, so that Christ's power may rest on me.

2 Corinthians 12:9 NIV

Sunrise

I haven't seen a sunrise since I retired, no joke. That's intentional because I love to sleep. I will attempt to describe what my soul feels about the sunrise. My plan to drive around the country on vacation was at the top of my bucket list. We jumped in the car, and off we went. The car ride and conversation were terrific. We made quite a few unplanned stops, talked to many who were doing as we were, and exchanged topics and findings uncovered along the way.

Many neon lights filled the air, advertising what was open, closed, for sale, types of entertainment, different brands of products, food, and more. It helped us find our way with road directions and lodging. In this case, the light was a good thing. Most would agree with me. Sometimes there is not enough light, and it creates fear or uncertainty.

For example, at my age, it is more comfortable for me to do daytime driving because of the glare from headlights approaching me on a pitch-dark road. Add that to the tiredness that comes earlier in the evening; you have a recipe for a dangerous nighttime drive. The technology installed in cars today that allows you to see the position and angles of the upcoming road helps, but more is needed. Light removes danger and scary situations, setting the stage, most mornings, for the most beautiful; take your breath away sunrises.

I have missed seeing the sunrise early in the morning and promised myself to catch several of them on our trip. We asked the hotel operator for a wake-up call and left the curtains open part way so we would see the light trickling in as morning came.

As the sun appeared, covering the entire horizon, light deepened with a brightness that could almost blind you. This magnificent sight was beautiful. It reminded me of how I felt when I first saw it as a child. I stood there in amazement. It was marvelous to see the different light tones that filtered and ate away the darkness with light patterns similar to the pastel shades in a box of crayons. It's as though someone had painted the sky with a blood-like pallet and some mustard wash. The glow was intense, and as more of the sun came into view, the tones appeared to be more thinly applied. A warm, soft hue that could be felt on your face. The sky, like that of a new baby girl's blanket, welcomed you to the new day.

There were a few straggly clouds, and as the light formed around them, they became more profound, darker, and heavier, not marshmallow-like or fluffy. A large portion of the sky was painted with a pallet that seemed to come from an explosion of a large amount of round, fuzzy, juicy, squishy fruit. As the sun inched its way further in the sky, the brightness on the infinite horizon reflected the landscape's vastness and the heavens' expanse. As particles in the air mix with large amounts of light fractures, the blood-like hue makes your eyes widen with a smile on your face and warmth in your heart; you say, "ahh." An old myth states that sailors believe a blood-like sky in the morning warns of weather danger ahead and that the blood-like sky in the evening is a sailor's delight. This fantastic sight couldn't possibly represent impending danger.

The Bible states that God destroyed the earth with a tremendous global flood and promised Noah no more global floods. He set His bow in the sky to remind us of that promise. This bow has seven schemes of light that change with the amount of filtered light pouring through the sky, giving us what we call our Rainbow. Many of the mixtures of light in the sunrise are representations of light tones in the Rainbow. These light schemes create tones, from deeply intense to blush, depending on the sun's position. When the sun clears the horizon and is positionally higher in the sky, the concentration of light shrinks from covering the entire horizon to just the circumference of the sun itself. At this point on cloudless days, you could only see the sky, faintly washed with berry juice, surrounding the sun. Each sunrise is unique and always seems more beautiful than the one before. I can't wait to see the sun rise again tomorrow morning.

Letter from Home

My Uncle Buster was a hilarious man. He had lots to talk about and a talker he was. After I became an adult, I visited him and his family. We spent many hours together at his kitchen table, talking about the job I had and the locations the job carried me to. He was enthralled by the work and travel I did for my career; there were many questions and discussions. He worked for the railroad and through his job, traveled and moved around as well. Uncle Buster had great adventures in Memphis, New Orleans, Chicago, and many other train stops because he could travel for free when he had time off. His stories had history and intrigue, making them so exciting that I couldn't stop listening and learning. He would tell me things about his childhood in the south and the migration to the north.

As the primary cook in his family, he was always cooking up something. Any day I stopped by, he would catch me as I went in the living room to talk to my aunt and entice me to come in the kitchen by saying, "I made some....... come and get some." His mom, my grandmother, was a fantastic cook and taught him everything he knew about cooking. Give him anything, and he could turn it into a feast.

No one could select a perfectly sweet ripe watermelon like he could. He said, "a good one was like getting a letter from home." Ever since then, I call watermelon a *letter from home*. I will tell my daughter to pick me up a *"letter from home,"* and she knows what that means. Now the whole family refers to it that way. Before I would leave, he would say, "I am making some ....tomorrow, come by and get some." Most often, I did. I was enamored by him and enjoyed talking to him, and I learned a lot. These talks inspired me.

Most of his children have gone on to glory except Margie. I keep up with her son Kelly and check on her from time to time with him. I hear from Kelly, Wendell or Theresa, and sometimes Chantel to keep me updated on Margie and her family.

Train to Remember

$\mathcal{P}$lanning was in place to start my train trip to visit my daughter Tai-Tanisha and her family in Alabama. The ride would be more than twenty-four hours. My friend Mary, Tai's mother-in-law, decided we would make the trip together.

Somehow we also got the wise idea of taking our great-granddaughter Ava'Marie with us. My daughter had never met her granddaughter in person. Mary and I are seniors. Ava'Marie was fourteen months old. What in the world caused us to think we could take a fourteen-month-old baby on a train trip that was more than twenty-four hours long?

We left early one morning before daybreak. The train was on time, and the upper cabin was very crowded. We were downstairs where the seniors belonged. That also made it easier to move around with the baby. Ava'Marie was a good baby. At her age, she did not need to purchase a ticket; she could ride for free. I decided to buy her a ticket anyway to guarantee her seat. Otherwise, she would have to sit on one of our laps if the train was full of paying passengers. That was not going to work for the distance we were traveling. There was no crying but lots of smiles, plus she slept quite a bit.

The train's movement was like a good rocking chair. We had all the formula, water, wipes, change of clothes, food, and diapers needed. She was in a carrier that made it easy to move around with her. We only did a little moving around. Mary watched her when I needed to get up, and I watched her when Mary needed to get up. The train was steady, and you could hear the constant sound of the wheels on the tracks. Riding the train is relatively peaceful, not hurried, but calm. Workers would come around to see if we needed anything. Everyone wanted to see the baby.

We changed trains in D.C. with nearly a half-day layover. There was time to go out and see some of the capital city, but with a baby in a carrier and two old ladies carrying it, that was not to be that day. "Can you envision that?" What a sight that would have been. Maybe we would have made the news.

Finally, the time for boarding the second and final train came. We were some of the first to board. You know how they treat older people, let them on because they are so slow. Otherwise, they will hold up progress. I was okay with that thinking. Just get me on so I don't have to wait in the crowd when they start pushing and shoving. Once seated, we got Ava'Marie unwrapped and comfortable as we reclined our lounger. We had the snacks we wanted but planned to order the train dinner to be brought to us by the staff. Everything went as planned. We had a good night.

In the morning, we arrived in Atlanta, where many people were getting off and on, which did not affect us. We sat and watched the madness. Ava'Marie was doing well and was still happy. In a few hours, we would arrive in Birmingham. My daughter and her husband were headed to the station to pick us up. Their trip to Birmingham by car was about four hours.

The train arrived on time. We allowed most of the passengers to get off first so we would not be run over by the traffic. When we got off we put all our bags on a push cart and headed to the waiting room. Tai-Tanisha and Michael were a short distance away. We sat in the waiting room and began to watch the television screen above us, and we were shocked at the news of a terrible school shooting. We knew nothing because we had been on the train without communication for twenty-four hours. We were mesmerized by the horrific news and prayed for all involved, especially the children, parents, and school staff.

Soon our ride arrived, and we hugged and kissed, and the baby was taken from us and given lots of hugs and kisses as well. Tai-Tanisha had never seen her grandchild until now. We stopped for lunch before heading to the house. That would still be about three hours. Mary and I needed to stand and move around because we had been sitting way too long. No one expected us to go that far with a baby and arrive without a hitch. Even now, everyone shakes their heads and laughs at the bravery of Mary and me to endeavor such a trip at our age.

Stuffin' vs Dressing

My mom and I always went to Atlanta for family dinner on Thanksgiving. When we arrived, Cousin Ida had already prepared most of her dishes. The day of the dinner, she realized she had forgotten something she needed to complete a dish. We ran to the store to grab it. We talked about the stuffing on the way, and she said, "I do not like stuffing." I said, "you made it yesterday!" She assured me that it was dressing, not stuffing. Back and forth we went with the stuffing versus dressing fight.

I decided to ask the shoppers in the store what they thought. With my invisible microphone, I walked up to shoppers, strangers no less, and asked if they had a minute to answer a question. Each shopper agreed. I asked, "do you make and eat stuffing or dressing?" Each shopper was asked the same question. Most, if not all, answered "dressing."

Some of the shoppers asked me, "what was the difference?" I explained, "that they were the same. Northerners called it stuffing, and southerners referred to it as dressing." Their understanding was that stuffing was only inside the bird. I told them my mom filled the bird, and the rest went into a large rectangular pan. The same ingredients and preparation went into each version. After much discussion, all agreed it was the same thing. It just depended on where you were brought up. The store manager was probably about to toss me out for being a distraction to shoppers in his store but decided to see what all the fuss was about. I even asked him the same question. Smiling, he gave the same answer the shoppers did, "dressing." But now they all understood it made no difference what you called it.

Cousin Ida probably asked herself why she brought her crazy cousin to the store to create such a ruckus. Ida thought, "never again is she coming with me, even though it was fun to see all those people speaking into an imaginary microphone and taking time to play along with my cousin."

Airplanes

As a young girl, I was most intrigued by gazing up into the sky, wondering about all I saw, imagining how everything came to be and how it all tied together. The clouds seemed to form actual shapes of things I knew, like animals, toys, and people. I believed they formed messages and someone somewhere could decipher them, and I was trying to do the same.

Occasionally, I would spot an airplane. How did they stay in the sky, and how did they get there? The sun was blinding if you looked right at it. You could only look for a moment, or your eyes would burn. The sky went as far as you could see with no end in sight, apparently meeting the land at the farthest point. Did the sky touch the ground? No one knows. Where is the end of the land? If I could go there, I would find out for myself where the sky touches the ground.

Looking into the sky in the daytime was much different from looking at night. The sun was gone, and the moon was out with many stars, some big and some tiny. We learned in school some of the shapes formed by stars. Where do they go during the day while the sun is out?

One day as I was playing, an airplane appeared in the sky. It looked tiny and moved slowly. How can that plane stay up there and not fall to the ground? If you threw a paper airplane in the air, it would swoop around and fall, crashing to the ground. Why wouldn't that big heavy metal plane fall? Who is flying the plane, and who is on the plane? What's going on in there? Can they see me, I thought, as I waved? Are they waving back? I can't tell. I was not afraid that the plane would fall on me because I could run fast and get out of the way. But I wasn't sure if they could throw something out the window that would drop on me. Yuck, that would not be good.

Riding in an airplane must surely be fun. Vowing that one day I would go on an airplane and look out of its window and see a young girl waving at me from the ground, staring up at the plane like I was doing. No one I knew had ever been on a plane. The only information I had came from a children's book with animated figures that scarcely gave a realistic view of the events and details of airplane travel. Everyone must be sitting still along the inside, secured by ropes, close enough to talk with each other but not to touch. From that day forward, whenever I saw or heard a plane, I would stop and stare at it until it was out of sight, always waving and wondering if they could see me.

Each plane had a different emblem and color. I guess that meant something. Even in my bed, I always heard planes flying at night. How could they see where they were going and how to get back on the ground in the correct city? Hopefully, they wouldn't crash into another airplane. Would they have to stay up there until daylight?

Once I saw a movie that showed the inside of a plane. The people were dressed up fancy and seated in comfortable seats eating and drinking. Wow, that was cool; how amazing. The ladies wore beautiful dresses, hats, and gloves. The men had suits with ties, and all of them wore hats. A waiter walked through the aisle, getting things for each person to enjoy. Everybody had a choice of meals for their dinner. It looked incredible. Could you imagine food with cutlery, drinks, and ice while flying? I have never eaten at a restaurant, but I know what they were like.

Eating while riding on a plane must be like eating at a restaurant with a flight attendant serving you. That's it, and I have to find a way to get on a plane. That would take care of two things, eating at a restaurant and being served while flying on an airplane. The movie showed the people sitting and eating but not where and how they got on or off the plane. Obviously, more research is needed. Maybe I will go to the library tomorrow, I thought. At least now I know they are not sitting on the floor tied with rope. How ridiculous was that?

Italy

The day has finally arrived. It has been a long time coming, and we didn't sleep much last night. Everything is crossed off my to-do list, and every outfit is matched and neatly folded in sets. My daughter has coordinated all of my grandson's clothes since she knows I have been known to get the outfits wrong every time. Everything from underwear to socks was folded together so I couldn't make a mistake. I'm not usually this organized but come on now, ROME? We have to look good every day. Tomorrow, Mikey and I will be in Rome. This is our first time abroad and is the most senior item on my bucket list.

We made it to the Pittsburgh airport in plenty of time, through security in record time, and finally to the departure gate. Hum, there is a buzzing and a crowd at the gate. No one was making any announcements, so we just parked ourselves and waited. I called my friend Marsha in Detroit, who is traveling with us for the second leg of our trip. We can hardly believe it. We are pinching ourselves over the phone to see if this is REAL. Shortly, it was announced that we are changing gates. That's always so exciting, you think?

The departure time is now a concern. We have yet to begin to act like we will board anytime soon. Finally, there is another announcement, The weather caused the plane coming in from Atlanta to be delayed, which is our plane to Detroit. Uh, don't they know it's imperative to make this flight so we can make the connection leaving Detroit? I called my friend in Detroit again; this time, the concern in my voice was unmistakable. We both began to "wish" the plane in from Atlanta. You ask, "How was that working for you?" Answer: not well. Then we resorted to praying. Actually, that should have been the first step.

The Detroit flight began its initial boarding process; I'm still optimistic. The flight time to Detroit is less than an hour. If there is a delay, intentional or otherwise, we can still make it. Hopefully, some delay on their end will hold up the plane just long enough for us to make it. My friend Marsha is not sure what to do. We talk again; I believe there will be a last-minute arrival and a run to catch the plane being held for us.

Reality check, we are not leaving. We are not going to Rome today. We are crushed and deflated, and I can hardly breathe. The last plane out of Detroit to Rome for today is now. I called my friend again, delivered the bad news, and suggested she go without us. We already paid for our hotel, et al. I told her to go; we would catch up tomorrow. She was somewhat apprehensive, not knowing how she felt about being in another country alone, but her cooler head prevailed. She went WITHOUT US. Mikey, my grandson, was as calm as can be. He didn't fully grasp what "was not" going to happen tonight. An announcement came with "Good News." They are scheduling a subsequent plane to Detroit in an hour, the storm has subsided, and our plane from Atlanta is airborne. Great, our plane to Rome is also airborne.

We, of course, took the flight to Detroit later that evening, all the while looking out the plane window to see if we could spot the flight to Rome going in the opposite direction. If we did, what good would that have done but make us more sad? We missed the flight by less than an hour. There was no way we were chancing that same situation and disappointment happening the following evening. We were going to be in Detroit this time tomorrow. On arriving in Detroit, we inquired about our luggage and whether or not we had to collect it or if they could hold it for the same flight tomorrow. We were told to leave our luggage for tomorrow's flight. It would be safe. (BIG MISTAKE).

Tomorrow came, and all cylinders were working. Thank God we were on the plane and on our way to Rome in first class, can you believe it, first class? All is well in the world. Yesterday's misstep was only a little memory now. We ate, drank, watched whatever movie we wanted, and were pampered, as was the norm for first-class passengers. Who cares about that plane that the storm held up out of Atlanta? We are on our way to Rome, "first class."

We arrived safely; our eyes were taking in everything. After having our passports stamped, we approached the baggage claim area amid a wave of hundreds of passengers who all seemed to speak different languages. We looked through mounds of luggage, and as the carousel cleared out, we were surprised to find that our luggage was not there. Oh yes, the luggage that the Detroit airport assured us they would hold for the next day's flight did not make it. They searched and found not one piece of our luggage.

The only thing to do was to go forth to experience our exciting trip without our luggage. We would not miss another moment of the most exciting adventure of our lives, luggage or no luggage. If we had to wear the same outfit for the entire three weeks, I was ok with that. The pictures we took would only make our family and friend question how much we saw in one day since we would be wearing the same outfit in all the photos.

PS We did not get our luggage back until the day before we came home (three weeks later). However, this was the most fantastic trip ever, even without our luggage. We had the best excuse to shop until we dropped.

Pinch Me

I don't know how I did it, that is, planning and getting ready to move to New York without a s.n.a.f.u. There was no internet back then or personal experience to help prepare me for New York. God planted the thought in my head and worked out all the details. It had to be Him. I worked out a timeline and found names of places for young ladies to stay that were safe and affordable. Then I would purchase my plane ticket. I had never been on a plane, I thought this would be super. I could not wait to get on the inside of the plane.

Before I left home, I contacted my cousin Ernestine who lived in the Bronx section of New York, and invited me to stay at her place. That was good news since I did not know anyone else in the entire city and state. Also, I did not have to find and stay in a facility for young ladies who had no other living quarters. Plus she was family.

All in all, much planning went into this move. Of course, my mom did not want me to go. She knew the type of place New York was and the kinds of people I could run into, and she tried her best to discourage me from going. Actually, she had lived there herself for a short while when she was young. There was a determination in my inner being that knew I had to go. My life at home had been quite serene, and I had not had much exposure to the fast-paced world. When I left home, the adult age to go to clubs, bars, and entertainment places was twenty-one (I was not twenty-one yet). In New York, the adult age was only eighteen for those establishments. Knowing what I know today, no wonder she was concerned.

Pressing on, I asked my Aunt Bea to take me to the airport, and she agreed. The next day she advised me that she would not be able to take me to the airport. My mom must have threatened her to within an inch of her life if she took me. She agreed to take me downtown to the bus station because an airport bus left downtown regularly. That would work.

The day arrived for me to leave, and mom continued to try to get me to change my mind. My aunt, mom, and I left for the bus station and found my bus ready to board. Mom went to the bus with me, still trying to change my mind. I sat in the first seat; the driver had yet to get on. Mom talked and talked. Inside, I was trying not to listen but could not help it.

I kept telling myself, "hurry up, driver, get on the bus so we can go." It seemed he would never come. I was exhausted from listening to all my mom said and was finally thinking that maybe this was not a good idea. I told her that she had to trust that she raised me well and could count on me to apply all she and the family had taught me. I even asked, "if things don't seem to work out, is it ok for me to come back home?" She said, "absolutely." I was about to give up and get off when I finally saw the driver on his way to the bus. Five more minutes, and I would have gotten off the bus. Oh, how my life would have been different. We said our goodbyes, or so longs, and mom got off, the driver got on, and we left. Both of us were crying a river.

New York, New York, Laguardia Airport. Never in my wildest dreams have I encountered so many different people, most of whom I could not understand what they were saying. They did not look like the people I grew up with. Where did they come from? Were they coming or going, and where to? The signs were in familiar letters but made words I had never seen or couldn't pronounce.

Everybody was in a hurry, going where? Only heaven knows. I stood there trying to determine what I wanted. Before you could count to five, several people and luggage would bump you or cause you to almost topple over. No one said excuse me or sorry. The best you got was a scowl from many that made you feel it was your fault that they ran into you. Often I heard words that accompanied a look that made me, without a doubt, know that a curse word followed. Until I looked up and saw the large bright, colorful sign that said, "Welcome To New York's Laguardia Airport," I wasn't sure if I was still in the USA.

Men and women stood in the luggage area holding signs with the names "Joseph Williams," "Marvin Cohen," "Ansonia Bristle," "Meyers Co," "Linda Smith," "Ford Motor Co," and others. Where was the person who was to hold my name? Were they late? Did something happen to them, or was I not expected? Someone should have known I was coming; after all, I did make a reservation. I wanted to shout and ask, "is anyone looking for me?" But I didn't; I was afraid. I ambled along, trying to stay on my feet and not get crushed as I made my way along the corridor to the baggage area. It was a long walk. I wanted to be thinking about my plane ride and how I had so long wondered about air travel. But, now I just wanted to get to my luggage and at the same time, stay on my feet.

I got close to a wall for protection as I looked at the baggage carousel and the number on my claim ticket. I can identify my cream-colored Samsonite luggage from here. Little did I know that so many bags looked exactly like mine.

Before leaving home, I remember being told, "don't look up in amazement at the tall buildings, don't wear a camera around your neck, don't appear lost (even if you are), don't ask just anybody for directions, and don't look confused." These are clues to the "wrong people" that you are a prime target to rob or take advantage of. I allowed most people to claim their bags before I ventured closer to the baggage carousel for fear of being crushed. These people were all rude.

When I arrived at the carousel and collected my luggage, I could have been robbed, conned, beaten, or killed. Thank God there were no "wrong people" in the airport that day.

I took a deep breath and realized I had made it. My luggage is with me.

SIDE NOTE: (YOU MAY FIND ANOTHER LUGGAGE STORY NOT SO SUCCESSFUL IN ANOTHER CHAPTER)

Now, if I can get to the door, I can find a taxi to take me into the city. I have the address I want. Hopefully, one will be willing to take me. There were so many people. I should have kept them from getting their bags first. The cabs may all be gone. Then what?

When I stepped outside, many men screamed and tried to get my attention while beckoning for me to come to them. Each man was standing at the head of an endless line of yellow cabs. I had never seen so many taxis, much less all in one place. Each one was vying for my business. "You need a cab?' Come, come. Their English was poor, but I knew they wanted my money and me in their cab. I picked the closest one. They loaded my luggage, I got inside, gave the address to the driver, and we quickly sped away. When I say quickly, I mean quickly. I hope he understood me. I was having a hard time understanding him.

The driver blew the horn endlessly, darting in and out of traffic and lanes. A license was posted on the plexiglass barrier between the driver and me. It had his photo, name, address, date of birth, license number, issue date, and expiration date. I kept trying to sound out his name, to no avail. I wasn't sure if the wall was there for his protection or mine. There was a slot under the barrier wall for the exchange of money. There was no way for the two of us to contact each other inside the vehicle.

Occasionally, the driver tried to converse with me, but again I could hardly understand him, and there was that barrier wall between us. He had a dark complexion but did not speak good English. He was not born here. He repeated what I said, I nodded, hoping it was right. The cab was musty, and the seats were black with several spots that may have been ripped at some point, but someone taped those spots with black electrical tape to prevent further damage.

I looked at the license posted to see the dates to determine if this was a new driver because the ride was fast and jerky, and I wanted to know if we would make it to my address. We changed lanes so often and abruptly that I was sure he would get in an accident. All of the drivers drove equally as bad. I held on tight to the seat. There should have been life preservers available. (This was before there were seat belts.)

Because of New York taxi drivers, I now understand why seat belts were created. I don't recall telling the driver I had a specific time to get there, but he was sure I would arrive on time. Believe it or not, I was still alive when I got there, pinching myself to be sure. The driver told me the amount to pay. I couldn't understand him, but looking at the meter was good enough for me to piece together what he was saying. I paid him and gave him a generous tip. He put me and my luggage on the curb and recklessly sped off to once again put fear in his next fare.

My cousin Ernestine showed me around and explained everything about New York: subways, dirty hot dog man, ethnic communities, shopping, and entertainment places. I had never gone to a laundromat to do laundry. Don't know if I even knew about them. There was an overwhelming amount to take in about New York, and Ernestine made the transition easy. Without her, I could still be standing on that curb with my suitcases. Thanks, Ernestine. I love you.

1994

Nineteen Ninety-Four was a significant year in which tremendous achievements were made, and remarkable history occurred in our world, both good and not-so-good. For example, Nelson Mandela was elected the first Black president of South Africa. Two blockbuster movies debuted, "The Lion King" and "Forrest Gump." If you are an avid sports fan, surely you will allow me to take you back to the most prolonged work stoppage by all major league baseball players in sports history, resulting in the cancellation of the highly revered World Series for that year. This was the first time the series would not be played since 1904. Due to the cancellation, there must have been an ample supply of hot dogs, popcorn, peanuts, beer, and "Cracker Jacks" on hand, hopefully not kept in a shed to be used the following year. Yuck! I wonder what could have possibly become of all that?

In the tech world, communication was not as we know it today. Young people, especially millennials, would fare poorly with the following statistic. Through the early 1990s, cell phones mainly functioned for business and only in a minimal way. In 1994, there were 67 mobile phones for every 1,000 people in Britain. The United States was just ahead of the British by a small margin. A decade later, by 2004, there were more mobile phones than people.

If you tried to do something exciting for young children, they would appreciate it. You think? Not always so. Let me take you back to one trip that made me realize how wrong I was in my thinking.

My daughter and her husband went away for a celebration. I offered to assist them by keeping their two young boys and baby girl for a week to ten days, silly me. My sister Emily was with me. We had the grand idea to take the children on a road trip, first to Delaware, then Baltimore, Washington D.C., and finally to New York City, before returning home to Pittsburgh. The boys were five and two years old. The baby was three months old. I was not a stranger to them or a seldom-seen grandparent, they knew me well. In other words, we were very familiar and comfortable with each other, and the children were well-behaved. "I got this," I said.

Before we started the trip, much trash had accumulated from the festivities around the celebration, and trash day was not for several days. That last weekend, had lots of family and friends in and out of my house; thus, lots of trash accumulated. Of course, we did not want to leave the trash in eighty and ninety-degree weather during June in a stuffy basement for a week or more. I came up with the bright idea to put the big black trash bag in the car and drop it off in one of the many dumpsters at my mother's apartment complex.

In the car were the two boys, Rafael and Carlos, the baby, Michelle, Emily, myself, luggage, three car seats, and the big black trash bag. We drove about twenty-four miles to mom's. The trash was quite fragrant, and we couldn't wait to get it out of the car and into the dumpster. Don't forget that this is June, and it was pretty warm.

When we arrived at mom's, we explained about the stinky garbage left over from the celebration. Getting a smirk and a grunt from her, we dropped off the big black trash bag of smelly garbage in the dumpster, said goodbye to mom, and off we went. Her look said far more than anything she could have said. Mom was not brave enough to travel with us on this long car excursion with three children, a smart lady. She probably imagined all sorts of things with the three small children, potty breaks, food breaks, crying, arguing, the heat, and who knows what else. Smiling sheepishly, she wished us well, turned, and went into her building. I hate to say it, but I realized she was "right on," when it was all over. There was no room for her in the car anyway, even with the big black trash bag gone.

Two days later, my daughter and son-in-law picked up the baby in Delaware, leaving us with just the two boys. I was so relieved that my sleep schedule would become closer to normal than with a three-month-old baby in tow. Now everyone could walk, go to the potty and feed themselves. Hurray!

The Baltimore Inner Harbor has a fantastic National Aquarium. Visitors came from miles away to enjoy this museum's scenery and aquatic life. There was a bright red ship, the "Chesapeake," decommissioned by the U.S. Coast Guard in 1971, after serving for 32 years. It is open for tours, and I thought little boys would enjoy this huge, incredible ship. Also in the Harbor is the USS Torsk submarine, painted with large jagged teeth to look scary, donated by the U.S. Navy as a memorial and a museum for touring. This, too, only interested my sister and me. The boys thought it ok, but I guess they needed to be older to receive from the experience what I thought they would get. As I wrote this piece, I pulled out my old camcorder and videos, and to my surprise, this trip was right on top. I smiled a lot as I watched and remembered this trip. Can't believe I found the video. Who knew?

In the water, lots of tourists were in paddle boats that were made out to look like dragons. Posted signs were all around the Harbor indicating that you could rent the paddle boats at the National Aquarium across the way. I still, to this day, don't believe my grandson could read all those signs at just five years old, but he indeed saw the boats and how to rent them, while he persisted in getting me to see them as well. Over and over, "Grandma, I want to get in that boat," he said. Each time it was more demanding. My answer was the same every time, "No, we are not going to ride today." Before my patience ran out, his did. He crossed his arms, tilted his nose up, and grunted, saying, "Fine, I am not going to be your friend anymore." The younger grandson was okay with everything we did. He did not know what he might have been missing. He was completely satisfied.

We never did ride the paddle boats. However, on the remainder of our trip, especially in New York, we had so much fun that I think he forgot about the paddle boats and not being my friend anymore. I am proud to say that he is still my friend. When I think of this time, I smile sheepishly and grunt in remembrance.

Domani

We boarded the train at the Florence station (that is Florence, Italy), where we would get the overnight train to Sicily. The train was over an hour late. There were bunk beds in our compartment three high. Mikey was on top, Ms. Marsha in the middle, and I was at the bottom. The room was so small that not even a mouse could fit in with us. There were racks up top to put luggage and a small sink and counter.

I was about to take the conductor out. Bam! He kept asking me for biglietti (tickets). We have ridden enough trains by now, to know what that was. So I showed him our biglietti's, and he was going to take them away. I said, "no, you can't take our tickets; we need them for other trips." We had purchased three-day Eurorail biglietti's, and this was only the beginning of the first day. We paid for them before we left home. I was not about to let him keep them. He kept saying, "domani domani." I kept saying, "no money; they are already paid for." He threw up his hand to his forehead and just said domani and took the biglietti from my hand, and I almost went off. I took them back from him, and back and forth we went. Finally, I begged him to find someone else who could speak English. He went away without the biglietti and brought someone else who knew no more English than he did. We were having a ticket war.

They left once again without the biglietti, and a third person came who could speak English. He explained to me what the conductor was trying to say. This is where knowing the language is essential. He said the conductor was trying to let me know that he would give back the biglietti tomorrow (domani). I will never forget that domani is tomorrow in Italian.

We learned that our train would get to the island of Sicily on a ferry, and I wanted to be awake to see that happen. We slept well, and in the morning, we woke up early to be ready to see the train put on the ferry. Never heard of a train on a ferry boat. He brought us our biglietti while I was in the restroom and gave them to Ms. Marsha. He probably saw me leave the compartment and decided to bring them while I was gone. He did not want to deal with me again. He also brought some thick black coffee, about two teaspoons in a cup, a roll, and some water. This was breakfast? It was. We did not get anything else.

We woke up in time to see them put the train on the ferry boat. We had our two teaspoons of coffee, roll, and water as they started to put the train on the right track to line up with the ferry track. We were at the station for quite a while. It took time to line up the tracks. We saw the surly conductor get off the train. Indeed the biglietti battle was enough for him. A different one got on. It must have been where he lived (Villa San Giovanni). After a few back-and-forth moves, the train was on the ferry. We got off the train and went up on the deck as we crossed over to Sicily. We took pictures, and there was a café to get juice, coffee, and other things. They even had American coffee. We bought a box of Ritz crackers and something to drink. The ferry sailed across the waters bridging the Tyrrhenian Sea (the western side of the mainland of Italy) and the Mediterranean Sea to Sicily.

After we arrived on the other side of the bay, the ferry lined up with the tracks there, and the train drove off the ferry into Messina,

Sicily. We were on our way once again. The train continued a couple more hours and arrived in Catania, where we were met by Rowland, our cousin, his wife Loretta, and son Elijah. We stopped for gelato and then drove to Rowlands's house at NAS Sigonella Navy Base, about 16 km from Catania. We stopped to pick up some things on the way to their house and relaxed for the rest of the day.

After dinner, Mikey played video games with Elijah, and we sat around talking. Rowland told us about some places and things to do in Sicily. He asked what we wanted to see, and we said we would leave it to him since he had been there almost three years. He did mention an overnight ferry ride to Tunisia, Africa, which was about €120 round trip which wasn't bad, but we did not have enough time. I wish we had known before we came. I sure would have liked to go to Africa, even if just to say I went to Africa. That would have been a fantastic story to tell. But we could not go. Not enough time. Maybe next time.

We got up early, ate, then sat around a bit before going to the Naval BX to shop for a few clothes since we still had not gotten our luggage. We watched a small part of the movie "The Godfather" so that it would be fresh and meaningful when we got to Savoca. We went through a town called Taormina. It is a beautiful beach town with stunning views.

Savoca is where part of the movie "The Godfather" was filmed. We sat at the table where Al Pacino asked for the girl's hand in marriage. We walked up the hill they walked to the church steps, where they took their vows.

The town had a catacomb with an exhibit of old dead people all dressed up and hanging along the walls. Not sure where they were going all dressed up. We decided not to go there. We found out later that many of these catacombs are in and around Italy. While in Savoca, we had more gelato. I got to sit in Al Pacino's chair and have my picture taken before leaving.

On the road again, we were finally in the town of Motta and dined at Valentino's Trattoria. The food was great. We had calamari, risotto (excellent), spinach, margarita (pizza), and other stuff. I learned that the servers do not come to your table unless you call them. I liked that. When you want burro (butter), you better say it right, or you might get Birra (beer).

Today we were off to the western side of Sicily. We went past an active volcano, Mt. Etna. It was not erupting, but we got some excellent pictures of smoke coming from the top. We drove to the town of Segesta, in the province of Trapani, where the Greek ruins were. We rode up to the amphitheater and saw many archeological items. The views from up there were beautiful. The amphitheater, along with other ruins located on top of Monte Barbaro, dates back to the third century B.C. The temple, for some reason, was never completed but dated back to the 5th century B.C. The people of Segesta were descendants of Troy, and it was ruled by Greeks, Romans, and Elymian people at one time or another.

After we left, we drove to Palermo, the point of western Sicily, near the meeting of the Tyrrhenian and the Mediterranean Seas. It was a large city—lots of people.

For lunch, we drove to a lovely medieval town called Erice. We walked up to the top and stopped to eat at an excellent outdoor trattoria. You see, all of the cities were built on the tops of mountains. It is said that they were built that way for protection from their enemies. When you drive at night, you see all the lights clumped together at the tops of the mountains. I need to know how they got all the stuff they needed to build on top of those mountains, using those narrow winding roads.

We left there and drove right through Trapani and took pictures and went to the salt marsh where we saw where they mine sea salt. Later we headed home, but only after some lady had a conversation with me about Facebook and Obama. They love President Obama.

We slept in the next day. We went to the Catania Aeroporto to check on the lost luggage in the afternoon. They told us the luggage was sent from Rome to Catania, but it has been sent back to Rome because no one picked it up. The number they had to reach us was the wrong number.

That night we had dinner in Catania at a ristorante named Camelot and then toured the town. I even got a chance to taste horse meat. Not bad; it tastes like chicken.

We drove to Messina the next day to see the Clock Tower. The tower is attached to a Duomo (Cathedral), and the inside of the Duomo is breathtaking. At noon, people gather to see the clock come to life every day. The Lion roars, the Rooster crows, and the Angels march around. It was cool. We took lots of pictures. Of course, we had some gelato.

Leaving Messina, we drove to Tindari (on the north shore of Sicily on the Mediterranean Sea, province of Patti) to see the Black Madonna. We were told that the Madonna was on a boat washed up on the beach and found by some fishermen. It was so beautiful that they turned it over to the priest; later, this Basilica (Sanctuary of the Black Madonna di Tindari) became its home. The beach below is called Mare Secco and is shaped like the Madonna praying. Tindari was built by the Greeks around 396 B.C.

The next day we once again checked on our luggage. Nothing. On our last night in Sicily, we went to Caltagirone, another medieval town, to walk around and see the lighting of the candle celebration. Everyone comes out at about ten pm (that is their dinner time). Folks get dressed up and come out late to have a good time.

We started getting everything ready for the overnight train ride to Rome. We went to the Naval BX to buy a few more souvenirs. That evening we boarded our train. Rowland gave us a suitcase since we had accumulated many things on the trip and still had not received our lost luggage. We said goodbye and took off to Rome. We had a small sitting room with six seats and two strangers for the overnight ride. Joy, joy!

PART 4

Christmas

But the angel said to them, "Do not be afraid. I bring you good news that will cause great joy for all the people. Today in the town of David a Savior has been born to you; he is the Messiah, the Lord."

Luke 2:10-11 NIV

Joy to the World

$\mathcal{B}$ing Crosby sings emphatically and melodiously in "It's The Most Wonderful Time of The Year." It's also "the hap-happiest season of all." Sound familiar? Many Christmas carols fill our spirits with joy and expectation for the entire month, usually beginning on Thanksgiving Day. This song is one of the most memorable ones. I walk around unconsciously humming and singing it almost everywhere. It's contagious. Cable channels play Christmas movies twenty-four hours a day between Thanksgiving and Christmas. My family calls them "sappy sweet movies" where you already know how they will end, and they are all the same. I love them and will binge on them anytime I can. It doesn't even have to be Christmas time.

I think the song's writer was cognizant of those "less fortunate," not having friends and family to spend those hap-happiest moments with. Maybe this was his way of bringing some joy to their spirits. For many (far too many), the season can't come and go quickly enough. There's not enough money for gifts, not enough food to eat, not enough friends and family, and mainly not enough hope in their lives to sing happy songs. Statistics have shown that many children don't have enough to eat or warm places to sleep and are surrounded by violence, dysfunction, and fear, equaling no hope. Also, there is more anxiety for those struggling with depression and high-pressure jobs during this season.

As a people watcher, I see things in the faces of everyday people and hear, with a third ear, some of the sadness and discomfort in our world. Many churches and ministries do significant outreach during this time of year to bring hope and joy to our community. The Angel Tree Ministry is where churches come together to bring hope and love to children who may not have enough and have a parent incarcerated. They do great work. My former church got me interested and participating in this ministry. Ms. Judy has reignited that flame in me to continue the same with her church here in Alabama.

Is it enough? Only God knows how to stir up what may have been lost by abuse, poverty, and abandonment, to state a few. While many others have so much more than they need or could ever use that could be put to good use in the hands of another. What do we have in our closets and basements that haven't been used for six months, a year, or longer? Would it not be put to better use by giving it away so someone could be warm, entertained, fulfilled, etc.?

In my heart, I know that Christmas is all about the birth of Jesus and his coming into the world as our Savior. This is the main reason for the season. It truly blesses my heart to be helpful in bringing joy to families and children during this season. As well as allowing my light to shine on the Savior for all to see.

Aloneness

Deep inside, during the holidays I feel a sense of aloneness, not sadness or depression, just alone. The feeling comes from losing old traditions and family members moving across the country or world. Some traditions acted like the glue that held the families together in love. I am open to developing new traditions if the old ones don't fit this new generation. Let's do it before all is lost.

The holiday is not just for ourselves. It has a definite "community" component to it. Putting up the decorations would not be such a job if done together. As a child, putting up the tree and decorations, inside and out, was almost as much fun as the expectation of Christmas morning itself. There were cookies baked, laughter, music playing, friends and family over, lots of tree-decorating food, and hot chocolate.

I will spend time with Jesus celebrating His birth, and sometimes I do that at home in my PJs. Has the world forgotten the reason for the season? By keeping the focus on what the season is really about, we can find hope and begin to spread hope to lives that so desperately need it. This is the hap-happiest time of the year but not in the way the world has grown to celebrate it. There will likely be serendipitous moments that I look forward to. I don't want to be sitting around with people texting and not communicating. I want to get out of my PJs, out of the house, and into a time of celebrating with friends and family. I miss that so much.

Family Gatherings

I have fond memories of large family gatherings that do not happen anymore in my family. The matriarchs who coordinated these beautiful memories are all gone. There were games, inside and out, lots of talking and laughing, and plenty of food. Relatives even drove in from out of town, and Uncle Buster and his crew were usually there in the earlier years. Friends were always there too, not just the children's friends but the adult's friends as well.

The younger generations today need more ties to close community and family events. They are often spread across the country and unable or unwilling to get home for some of the most memorable holidays. Their priorities are different.

At my daughter's house, they have almost always had the traditional Christmas meal, with different sides each year. Tom (turkey) would always be in the middle of the table. If I did the food, it would have an ethnic twist, which they like, but not for Christmas.

The older generation of women spent time together in the kitchen for all large family and friend events, with multiple generations working, talking, laughing, and, yes, sometimes bickering over the cooking. It was fun bickering. That is where the cooking skills you learned were put to the test by expert cooks like my grandma and mom.

Everyone got their assignment of cutting, basting, or whatever they assigned you. I liked being there to hear all the stories and maybe some gossip from the women as they prepared the meal. I learned more by watching what they did than by getting a class on doing that chore. That's just how it was back then.

Far too many young adults can't hold a conversation face to face for more than a minute or two, then back to checking text messages, etc. I would love to have large family gatherings again. Sadly I don't see that happening. What a daunting time in the life of many young people, evolving into closed communication, even with those closest to us. Maybe one solution could be to have all cell phones put in a bucket at the door when they enter, and let's see how much fun and laughter we can have. Of course, they will get them back on their way home.

There was such a good time to be had by all, and a tradition that I am sorry has gone from not only my family but many families. My wish is to bring that back one day.

We also had lots of friends over. Today it's just the family that lives there, no out-of-town family or friends. It can be restored, but it will take prayer, coordination, and willpower. I think it's worth it.I am sure my family would love it if they tried it.

The Parade

Somewhere in the not-so-distant past, I became paralyzed by the commitment to decorating for the holiday. Don't get me wrong; I love to see homes and stores decorated wonderfully for Christmas. When my daughter was young, we lived in New York. We did not miss going to the Macy's Thanksgiving Day Parade. I gathered seven or eight kids to take with us on the subway to the parade. One tradition we have kept over the years since we are no longer in New York is getting everybody out of bed to watch it on television on Thanksgiving morning.

Christmas has always been one of the most exciting times of the year. Remembering when my cousins, Valerie and Roslyn, wanted to go to the parade in person put a smile on my face. We always got up early to watch the parade on Thanksgiving. We did not live in New York when I was a teenager. My city had a local parade, but it was not as grand as the Macy's parade. Once mom said we could go and be there in person instead of watching our local parade on television. I was glad to be given the responsibility of taking my cousins to see the parade in person.

It was freezing cold, and we bundled up well and then some more. We put our bus fare in our gloves and headed to the bus stop. I had traveled on buses many times and knew the way. When the bus came, we got on and took our seats while carefully watching for the stop to get off.

After getting off, we walked and found a front-row spot where no one blocked our view. It was a long time before the parade began. We moved and jumped around to keep warm so we would not realize how cold it was.

Smiles came to our faces when we saw the first performers, some floats, and many bands. Everything was beautiful. The music was loud and put us in the Christmas spirit. Once the parade started, we did not think about the cold anymore. The parade lasted a long time. Finally, we saw Santa Claus at the end of the parade. It got louder, with kids screaming and clapping. Smiles were everywhere. Soon he had passed by, the parade was officially over, and the crowd started to thin out. We started walking towards where we would get the bus to return home.

At home, all I wanted was hot chocolate and a blanket. The girls were so excited to tell their mom everything about the parade. It was nice. I am glad we went. We had a good time.

Recently, dressing my house for Christmas has become a chore. My excuse is, "no one is going to see it but me." But I like driving around to see the decorations others put up.

Year after year, I did less and less decorating. A few years ago, I decided to do no decorating. My friend encouraged me to put a few things around the house and light a candle or two to please myself even if no one else would see it (Thanks, Bobbi). That was a job, and it stressed me out, but it worked. Even others who know my tentative nature about decorating started encouraging me earlier because they knew I would need to be puffed up again. Last year I surprised them and contacted my decorator, Pinterest, and saw terrific designs and decided to try some of them.

A few things got put around; a wreath was placed on the door, the table was set with holiday dishes, a table runner (that I made), and a centerpiece. I even added some large glittering snowflakes to hang from my dining chandelier and lighted garland to surround the entrance to the central part of the house from the hallway. A week later, I drug the tree and ornaments from the garage and put them up with the help of my granddaughter, Kristia. Everything looked great. But, "no one is going to see it but me."

One night in early December, I thought about taking it all down and putting it away until I was reminded of the celebration coming the week before Christmas, and I knew people would be coming over. I reluctantly left everything up. I had invited several ladies to join me for a Chat n' Chew.

Chat N' Chew

The occasion was just as it says: we chatted and chewed. The Chat N' Chew is a recurring event that hooked me in Pittsburgh. I was first introduced to it by Bobbi, and her amazing sister Michelle, affectionately known as Shelly. Arlene was a part of our group as well as Bea. Each time someone different hosted the gathering, ladies would come for the afternoon and evening to celebrate whatever we wanted to celebrate. We always met at Christmas time and usually, one other time during the year. We were asked to wear what is known as an ugly Christmas sweater during the holiday season. The host asked you to bring a side dish and, most assuredly, bring your most festive self.

I assigned my guests homework to bring to the Chat N' Chew. One year each was given a "bad boy" or "bad girl" of the bible to research and share with the group. Another time it was Jacobs's sons, and still another, it was parables of the bible. It allowed people to explore the character and possibly bring out something someone didn't know. We did not falsely fabricate the details but used our creative style to make each presentation more enjoyable. We made it fun by acting out our characters. I was in charge of the menu, which included appetizers and dinner for the celebration. There were prizes and a Secret Santa gift exchange at the end.

Typically the Chat N' Chew happens a few weeks before Christmas and occasionally one in the summer. Since moving South, our original group no longer does the Chat N' Chew, but I have introduced it to ladies in the South. They love it and always look forward to it. Friends in Colorado (Sheila) and Michigan (Marsha) love this event, too. We will do anything to celebrate Christmas. Just waking up and greeting each other with "Merry Christmas" works even when it is not the Christmas season. Even in the summer, ask Bobbi how that played out at Sheila's in Denver. It puts a smile on your face making for a good day.

Merry Christmas to all.

Nails & Gifts

Last year, the sisterhood had a contest on a group chat to see whose fingernail design decorations were the best. We would get our nails done at our favorite shop, take pictures, and share them with the group. Raelyn, my granddaughter-in-law, suggested having the men judge them and vote on which ones were the best. We would repeat this every couple of weeks when everybody got fresh designs. We used the winter holidays as inspiration for our designs. Raelyn coordinated this and arranged for the recording of the votes. I was sure my nails were the best, but I never won. This was a good Koinonia where we could all participate and were anxious to see the results. I hope we do it again.

That year was the first time we all decided to have a Secret Santa gift exchange. Our family is so spread out across the country that it seemed like a good idea to do Secret Santa. Trying to see how to work this out without anyone of us knowing each other's Secret Santa was cumbersome. Our good friend Shontel decided that since she was not in the family gift exchange, she would be our Secret Santa administrator. That worked out great. There was an amount set for gift purchases. Each person was to contact the Secret Santa administrator to find out whom they would buy a gift for and let her know when it was purchased and mailed. The administrator kept track of everything and did a fantastic job of keeping things secret. We want to have another go at it this year too.

Most Memorable Christmas....

Thinking back over my life, attempting to find a more unique Christmas than any other, was quite stressful. I was most definitely going to initiate a call to the therapist because I couldn't find just one Christmas that fit the bill. Don't get me wrong, none of them were terrible. Many were wonderful.

Lillie Solomon, my mother, was always the leader of the pack in our family as far as decorating, cooking, baking, and scheduling events at the family house. Everybody was always invited for dinner, I think. Some relatives just showed up with their kids to get good food without having to cook and show everybody what they got for Christmas. My mom did not have any friends who had children. They were a little too old for kids. Mom's friends were no fun for me when they got there. My dad always bought me a bike for Christmas, which I liked. My bike was stolen several times, so I had to keep getting a new one.

Every Christmas usually followed that same pattern. When I lived in New York and did not go home for Christmas every year. After getting married, I spent the holidays with my husband's family when I did not go home. If I thought my family was a little unusual, theirs was in the same boat as us. Puerto Ricans with a robust New York culture had different traditions from mine. I enjoyed them as I tried to understand the language, hoping they were not talking about me when sometimes they would break out into Spanish. I started to learn the language.

Tai-Tanisha was born on December 21, just in time for Christmas. She was the most beautiful thing that ever happened to me. She was my Christmas present that year. The kind of present that keeps on giving. Most of my daughter's adult years after she was married and had children were spent in other states, far from where I lived. Traveling each year from my home in the snow belt was interesting because I had to track the weather for a week to see when I could leave without running into a snowstorm. Driving was the most practical way to go since I had lots of stuff to take with me for the kids and family. One year I brought along Libya, a young girl I mentored. That was her first time going out of town. She participated in many holiday traditions with us that she never knew existed. I am sure it was her most memorable Christmas ever.

My grandchildren are all grown up. Christmas is still not exactly what I would like it to be to fit into the "The Most Memorable" category. Everybody wants to sleep as long as they can, nobody wants to invite friends over, dinner is served whenever it's done, most don't dress in festive wear, there is no snow where I live now, and I have to keep telling them I don't want any gifts. Nobody comes to my house, so why do I even put up decorations?

Can I deviate and tell you what my Most Memorable Christmas would be like? If you have seen the movies "This Christmas" with Loretta Devine and Chris Brown or "The Family Stone" with Craig Nelson and Diane Keaton, they probably hit the nail on the head. Both bring a deep sense of family closeness, and each cherishes friends, food, fun, and experiences unique drama. These families are somewhat eccentric and may even be called weird sometimes. But, all in all, they exude extreme love for one another and wait with excitement every year for each one to arrive to share this time. What meant the most was that everyone was together.

In those movies, the generations of women in the kitchen sharing but not always agreeing touches my heart in an extraordinary way. Everybody was cutting, mixing, frying, or doing what the leader is telling them to do to get the dishes to all come together and be ready at the same time. Like my mom did. It looked like the smells coming from their kitchens were fantastic, too. If you take a deep breath and hold it, while closing your eyes for a second, you can imagine those smells. These are my favorite movies. I have to watch them every year.

I remember as a child, Christmas music was playing while football was on the TV, and the men were doing their thing in the living room. The phone kept ringing, and the doorbell, too; lots of hugging and kissing. Laughter was everywhere and embarrassing stories of past holidays and some of the mishaps kept getting retold year after year. You know those stories most of us want to forget, but someone will always bring it up. Oh yes, your most embarrassing moment.

Everybody sat down for dinner at the same time. It's not just family. Friends are there to share in this special event as well. After dinner, small groups broke off to go to a club, play games/cards, watch movies, or go caroling. I want this time again, but it may be too late; it's probably gone for good.

The younger generations don't seem to want this type of holiday fare. Maybe I'm just dreaming or simply too sentimental. Some traditions must be maintained and passed down from generation to generation to keep the family memories alive and make new memories for the younger generations. They will have nothing to look back at, smile, and tell their children. Young folks today have a different sense of gathering. I am tired of hearing, "that was back in the day; people don't do that anymore." Maybe they don't but let's try it and see if it will catch on again. Try it; you might like it.

Submitting (under duress) to this new way of life, I will pull out my cell phone or tablet and play a couple of games while waiting for dinner. Who knows what time that will be? Too bad our younger generations won't be able to write about many of their most memorable Christmas moments, in their later years.

I thought I would need to get therapy to write this story. Each year I attempt to shut down and not put up decorations. What's the point? This is a new stage of life for me, and things will not be the same anymore. I get it. I may accept it one day. You think?

(I like the idea of everyone dropping their phone in the bowl when they come in for the holiday gathering so no one will be distracted from the main reason for gathering, to be with and communicate with each other.)

Through all the fun or not, laughter and food or not, keep in mind the main reason for the season, the birth of Jesus Christ our Savior. Merry Christmas to all of you.

PART 5

Tai-Tanisha

Trust in the Lord with all your heart and lean not on your own understanding; in all your ways submit to him, and he will make your paths straight.

Proverbs 3:5-6 NIV

Bubble Gum

In Brooklyn, N.Y., on busy neighborhood street corners, you could see a gumball machine sitting outside a barber shop, corner store, or market filled with colorful round gumballs. One only needed a penny to put in the slot, turn the handle, and down would come a sweet colorful gumball or two to enjoy. They were intentionally placed at eye level of toddlers and young children, calling them to stop, look and buy.

The neighborhood of Crown Heights in Brooklyn was always busy with people shopping at meat markets, shoe stores, laundry mats, grocery stores, dress shops, and barber shops. We lived about midway through the block on our street. There were barber shops on both sides of the street near the corner.

My daughter loved to take walks as a toddler. Living in a small apartment seemed cramped at times. Taking a walk right before nap time was always a good idea. It gave us some much-needed fresh air and prepared a toddler for immediate sleep on our return. After lunch, we bundled up, and off we went.

Saturday was my day off, and usually, I had several errands to run. The first stop was always the cleaners. On the way to the corner, in front of the barbershop, just outside the door, stood a gumball machine. My daughter was always such a good girl. I would have that penny ready to put in the machine while she turned the knob and held her tiny hand underneath the slot to catch the gumball. She was so excited. Off we'd go to the cleaners and other errands, holding each others' hands.

I would sometimes forget the penny rushing to get out of the house. The gumball machine always caught her attention as we passed. If I did not have a penny, I would attempt to explain that we could only get our gum once we were on the way home and had a penny. A sad little face would appear, but it was soon gone.

Whether it was sunny or snowing, the shop owners always remembered to set the gumball machines on the sidewalk. Maybe they thought that if people stopped in front of their shop to drop a penny in the gumball machine, the customer would come inside to spend more, but not so in our case. We dropped our penny, turned the knob, got the gum, and kept going. Besides, we were never going to need a haircut.

Week after week, time after time, we followed the same routine. If I said no, not today, she would tear up, try to balk, and make me get a penny out.

As the parent, I believed that a gumball machine would not rule me. Thinking I was in control, it soon became apparent that a battle was raging between me and the gumball machine. I was determined that I, the adult, was going to win.

When considering my strategy, I decided on a course of action that would be easy and fix everything. We left our apartment building, this time crossing the street in front of our door. We walked side by side, holding hands as usual, with my daughter on the inside. Hopefully, she would not see the gumball machine across the street once we reached the corner. Oh no, to my surprise, there was a gumball machine at nearly the same spot on the opposite side of the street from the original one. I did not even realize the convenience store had a gumball machine too. Here we go again; another drama was ensuing.

With lots of errands to get done, I surrendered the penny. No time for a child with an attitude, especially since we would also have to pass the gumball machine on the way back home. You could count on seeing a gumball machine either going or coming.

The following week called for a different strategy, but I needed help thinking of one. Today we were going for our walk and doing some errands. Bristling up, and trying not to be resentful, I decided to bite the bullet; THERE would be no gum today. I was determined that today we would leave and return home with NO GUM. All right now, I'm pumped! Feeling good about myself and the plan, let's do this.

Here we go, out the door and heading to the corner; so far, so good. There it is, the dreaded gumball machine. We had a discussion and agreed we would pass by it. (Discussing and agreeing with a two-year-old may have been optimistic.) Somehow we made it past the gumball machine. Turning the corner, we went in and out of stores and were doing great. Next, we stopped at the drugstore and the grocery store. Our errands are complete, and we are ready to head home. Never had I noticed a toy machine at the grocery store door. I refused to entertain a new challenge. "No," I said and left the store holding her hand, slightly tugging.

Just outside, my daughter lost her mind. She started screaming and wringing her hand, trying to separate herself from me. Her knees went limp, and down she went to the ground, a full-blown tantrum. No, she didn't! I don't know exactly where the thought came from, but I looked and saw I was only three doors from the corner. Our hands separated, and I kept walking, leaving her on the sidewalk. Glancing over my shoulder, I could see she was still on the ground and beginning to get up, looking for me. As I slowly turned the corner, I could see her clearly, and she was up and running toward me. I continued slowly walking. She caught up to me and took my hand. We did not miss our stride or say a word. We passed by the gumball machine and went straight home without any notice or mention of the gumball machine at all. I am feeling good. Winning is great.

Surely she must have realized in her tantrum that her mom, leaving her lying on the sidewalk, was crazier than she was.

She learned a valuable lesson that day and hopefully understood that having a tantrum would not get her whatever she wanted, and it did not change mom. She never had a temper tantrum about anything ever again (smile). I learned a valuable lesson as well. Consistency is imperative. No is no and when you start a cute thing, like carrying a penny and letting her put it in and turning the knob, was not so cute when you want to change the rules of the game. Oh, and one more thing, never make deals with a two-year-old.

PS: Today, I would probably have had the authorities knocking on my door later for abandoning my child on a busy sidewalk in Brooklyn.

Sleep

Sleep is a fantastic thing. Some people seem to wake throughout the night many times, breaking their REM sleep and then being sleepy all the next day. Unknowingly, some people get out of bed at night and walk around in or out of the house. This is called sleepwalking. Sometimes I can't get enough sleep; according to others, sometimes, I get too much.

As a child, I had rather strict bedtimes but never seemed to want to get up in the morning. When I left home and was on my own, I began staying up quite late but always got up in time to get to work early. Some days I had to drag myself out of bed. I have turned into the most joyful nocturnal person on the planet. Reading, sewing and projects come easier at night. I mean midnight. Why wouldn't I go to bed so getting up would be easier? To this day, that question is unanswered.

When my daughter was born, she was nocturnal as well. For the first four to four and a half years of her life, she would wake up for the two o'clock feeding, even after no longer requiring a two o'clock feeding. She would wake up and want to coo and play. I would not dare turn the light on for her to see me because she would never go back to sleep. She would wake up wanting to play, sometimes staying awake for up to two hours, which would mess up my morning. It became harder and harder to get up daily, even now. She messed me up for life.

Living and working in New York City meant that the subway was your primary mode of travel around town. I could sleep while standing and holding onto the stirrup on a crowded morning commute. As the subway train sped along at a rapid pace and slowly approached the next stop, much screeching and some deviation from the smooth ride would occur. When the subway train stopped, I would open my eyes and notice the name on the wall to see if it was mine, if not, back to sleep I would go. I never missed my stop.

Before retirement, my job required me to travel weekly, usually by airplane. Most days, I would get a morning flight leaving before seven to arrive at a meeting or client by about nine in another state and most often in a different time zone. Those early mornings messed me up even more. Frequent fliers had the opportunity to board first. While everyone else boarded, pushing and shoving things into the overhead bin, I would attempt to read while this chaos was happening. Unintended, I would fall asleep. I would find my book on the floor when we landed. I never saw the plane take off. I was always asleep by then. I slept soundly, not waking until the pilot announced over the PA system that we were preparing for landing.

Once, I woke up when the pilot announced our arrival and looked out my window to see an unfamiliar airport that I did not recognize. Somewhat frazzled, I asked the stewardess where we were. It turned out that the pilot received notice to make an unscheduled stop. I did not need to get off we were here for just a few minutes and then on to the stop I expected. You might think that would have deterred sleep, but it did not.

I remember when a young man sitting next to me on the plane talked about his first son. He had some hilarious stories, and we laughed about kids in general. Midway through our conversation, I fell asleep. When I woke up, he asked me, "how did you do that? You were in mid-sentence, and suddenly you were asleep." He had never seen anything like it.

Since retirement, my goal has been to sleep as long as possible, especially in the morning. Therefore, I can stay up late at night, and I do. I have paid my dues by getting up early first for my infant daughter, my grandson, and my job. I have earned it, SLEEP.

I Have Arrived

My husband Carlos and I traveled from New York to Michigan to help drive to Mississippi in "hot as heck" August while I was pregnant. My mom and Aunts Bea and Emma had not returned to Mississippi since they left over thirty years ago. My husband had never been to Michigan, and neither of us had been to Mississippi. It was quite a drive. We arranged to break up the journey by spending the night in Jackson, Tennessee, at a hotel. None of us had ever stayed in a hotel nor seen the inside of one. We did not know what to expect. Not one person I knew had ever been inside a hotel, that is, as a customer. We probably looked a little timid and did not ask for any extras. However, everything went smoothly.

Everybody went in and got ready for bed. I had seen enough movies to know what hotels were like. Nosy me, I wanted to go out and roam around, get ice and check out the pool. We dared not think about getting in it. That would undoubtedly have caused an interesting story for the evening news and possibly jail time. Remember, this was around the time the country, especially the south, was accepting new laws regarding integration. Some southerners are still uncomfortable with equal rights and services for all races.

Our entire stay was comfortable, and everything went well. I felt like a high roller. Do you realize that one of the highlight stories about our trip was the one about the hotel? I told everybody about it. This was a story I shared later with my daughter since she experienced it with me four months before she was born. Little did I know that in my work career, I would spend as much time in hotels as in my own home, for years.

Once we arrived in Mississippi, I was excited to see the stomping ground of my mother's growing up years and some of the still-standing landmarks of their time there. I saw where my grandmother worked as a cook, where they lived, the church, where they grew up, and other spots. We met some relatives whom I had only heard their names mentioned. It was a good trip, even though air-conditioning was non-existent everywhere. It was an eye-opening experience I am glad to have had.

The return trip was good, and we stayed at the same hotel on the way home.

November came, and on the presumed due date of my baby, I was admitted into the hospital because someone got their dates wrong or the baby heard about all of the happenings in the world and decided to delay its arrival. After spending two days in the hospital, we were advised that the baby was not due yet. "Go home, mom," I was told.

One month and a couple of weeks later, it was, of course, late at night. I decided it was time to go to the hospital for real this time. My husband was not home, but my mom was there. I thought I had gas, but I kept lying on the couch. Then more gas. What the heck, this was my first baby, "how did I know these were labor pains?" After complaining about having gas, my mom thought it was a good idea to start timing "the gas." Soon, she realized it was not gas and that we should prepare to go to the hospital and call my husband. He said he would be right there. The pains that I thought were gas were coming closer together.

We called a cab and prepared to leave. We told my husband to meet us at the hospital. The taxi came but did not want to take me because he was shouting that he would not have a baby born in his cab that night. Yuck, New York taxi drivers are so fickle. I pleaded, and finally, we were off to the hospital.

Carlos met us there as they began to prepare me for delivery. An IV would be good right about now; the pain was getting stronger. The exam showed it was not gas but labor, and we were told it would be quite some time until the baby came. That was not what I wanted to hear. I tried to sleep on and off. Finally, morning came. I could see daylight. The pain was worse. There was nothing I could do but wait.

On December 21, at twelve forty-five in the afternoon, we welcomed Tai-Tanisha into the world. Just four days before Christmas. She was so sweet and cuddly; I just wanted to hold her and hold her. I had originally picked out a boy's name because I thought that was what I was having. But I had a girl's name in the back of my mind. There were four babies in each nursery. Two moms in each room, one on the right side of the nursery and one on the left. The nursery with the four babies sat in the middle of the two mothers' rooms. There was a window separating our babies and us, but we could always see them. That was great.

Moms and babies came and left, and Tai-Tanisha and I remained. I believe I had about three different roommates during our stay in the hospital. Christmas day, we had lots of guests and a great dinner. We were still there. We stayed for over a week, and finally, we went home. Welcome home, Tai-Tanisha!

My daughter and her dad bonded quickly. As a toddler, they watched cartoons together, and he spent time spoiling her. She was indeed a daddy's girl. They would call me and say, "bring us some milk and cookies; bring us this or that." I was just there to serve.

In the end, I am so glad my baby was a girl.

Hide & Go Seek

Tai-Tanisha was quite humorous. We ran to the mall one evening just before closing. I peeked at a few sale items, and my daughter held my hand. I picked up an outfit and took a closer look at it. I dropped her hand for a moment. After a closer look, it was the wrong size. I turned to the round rack behind me where the other sizes were and selected a different one. The lady said I only had five more minutes before closing. Quickly I gave the item to the sales lady and reached down to get Tai-Tanisha's hand. There was no Tai-Tanisha. We were the only customers in the store since it was closing time. I called her name and rushed around every circular clothes display, but no Tai-Tanisha. The sales lady and another employee started looking also. Now I was frightened.

I believe the lady called security. All the time, I kept calling her. It had only been a minute, and no one else was near us in the store. My heart started racing, and I was getting scared. Where could she be? We got louder. One lady looked in the dressing room, and another looked in the next department.

Just as security reached us, I was still calling her and looking franticly, but still no Tai-Tanisha. Soon, I heard snickering from within the center section of the round clothes display rack. I yanked the clothes back, and she was, sitting on the floor laughing. She must have thought this was a game of hide-n-go-seek. I grabbed her hand, and she got up.

I hugged her and gave her a big kiss. The salespeople and the security were glad she was found. On the other hand, I was so happy to see her that I could not be mad at her antics.

We left and went straight home. In the car, we talked about how dangerous that could have been and how sad I would have been if someone had taken her. Over the years, we have remembered that story and laughed out loud. I told her the next thing was to get her a harness and leash. Which I later did.

Out on the Island

Just down the block from our apartment in Brooklyn, you could find several shops where you could buy everything you needed. We spent much time looking for and purchasing everything from soup to nuts. Tai-Tanisha, Carlos, and I were walking to the store when a man approached us and began asking for directions in Spanish. I did not speak Spanish at that time, but to my surprise, my husband answered him fluently. He could speak Spanish; who knew? He grew up in a house where that was the primary language, and I thought he probably understood it well but never thought he could speak it. Wow, now I had someone to help me learn.

Sometime later, I was able to meet his dad and his family. We started visiting them on Sundays on Long Island. Their primary language was Spanish, which I did not speak. The family would try to speak English for my sake. That's only until they became passionate about something, and they would immediately break into Spanish. I would say, "No, English or Spanish, English or Spanish?" They would say "sorry" and go back to English.

I decided that priority one was to learn Spanish at least enough to defend myself at his dad's house when everyone reverted back and forth between the two languages.

Eventually, I spoke pretty good everyday Spanish but learned to understand it even more. Today, I wish I had stuck with it. I even took a class here or there. I still understand a bit but not as much anymore since I am away from those who speak that language. Some of my grandchildren may embark on Spanish, and I will attempt to become fluent once again.

The Boat

Michael invited his mother Mary and I to go fishing in the Gulf of Mexico. We took the two younger children, Michelle and Mikey with us. Mary loves to fish. That was right down her alley. I wanted to go on the excursion, but I did NOT want to fish.

Fishing with mom as a child started off being fun. Mom and her friends liked going in the evening when it cooled off, fishing overnight, and going home the next day around noon. Trying my hand at fishing was fine for a while, but then I fell asleep in the car while they fished for the rest of the night. I was thoroughly done with the fishing thing.

We planned to spend the entire weekend. Michael had two tents. Mary, Michelle, and I stayed in the one tent; Michael and Mikey slept in the other. Michael made a campfire and cooked burgers, hot dogs, and marshmallows. Michelle collected some sticks for us to use to put our marshmallows on. She spent so much time taking the bark off and then washing the sticks until we just ate the marshmallows like they were. She must indeed be her mother's child (smile). Michelle has never more exemplified her mother than at that moment. Before dark, we went out for some snacks. There were cold cuts, bread, drinks, and other things in the cooler. We did not get hungry.

When it was time for bed, actually, there was no bed; Michael blew up two air mattresses and put one in each tent. Nearby was a wash facility where we could wash up and change into our PJs. Michael zipped us in for the night after we somehow got down on the ground and crawled onto the air mattress inside the tent. No one was going to get in, and we were not going to get out. Hopefully, no one will need to go to the bathroom.

Our vehicle had a hitch on the back, that we used to tow Michael's boat to the campsite. Sometimes we fished on the dock, and sometimes we went out in the boat. Not caring much for the actual fishing, I liked the boat ride. Mary, Michael, and the kids fished. I took in the sights. Some water splashed over the sides of the boat as we motored along. No one cared that we got a little wet.

Michael asked his mom if she wanted to drive the boat. She shook her head and declined. Next, he asked me, what do you think my answer was? Oh yea, sure. I got up from my seated position and sat where I could steer. He instructed me on the boat's mechanics and what I needed to do to speed up, slow down, turn, and stop. With a massive smile on my face, I drove the boat. I had never been in a personal-sized boat, much less driven one. We were in the Gulf of Mexico. This was way cool. I did not capsize us or anything terrible. However, there was a boat that was much larger than us that created a fair amount of waves when they passed us. Compared to us, one would have thought it to be as large as a cruise ship, but it was simply a larger personal boat. No problem, I held steady, plus Michael was always right there. He would be ready to take the wheel immediately if necessary. What a lovely day we had. I will always remember that.

Later we had to take the boat out of the water and connect it back to the boat trailer. That took a little maneuvering. If I remember correctly, Michael pulled the boat close enough to the dock for me to climb out and get the truck. I backed the vehicle and the trailer almost into the water at his instruction, far enough to allow him to attach the boat. Then I drove forward until the whole boat was out of the water. There is a first time for everything. Who knew I would like this so much? Next time we go fishing, I am definitely driving the boat.

We spent another night at the camp. The following day, before going home, we toured an aviation museum at the campsite before leaving. I learned a lot about the exhibits and the lighthouse. That was one of my best vacations. Thanks, Michael, for the memory.

PART 6

Mom

Carry each other's burdens, and in this way you will
fulfill the law of Christ.

Galatians 6:2 NIV

Rain Barrel

I remember a story my Uncle Buster told me that he recalled from when he was a kid. My mom and her sisters were supposed to watch him while their parents went to town. Some friends came to their house, and the girls decided to get the rain barrel next to the house, fill it with water from the well, and use it for swimming. Just in case you might not know, rain barrel water is clean rainwater that rolls from the roof when it rains. They used it for bathing and boiled some for cooking and sometimes drinking. It certainly was not for swimming. Nevertheless, the girls decide to swim in the barrel.

Uncle Buster, their younger brother, was on the front porch since he was not permitted to swim in the barrel with the girls. Suddenly, he spots his mom and dad walking home on the road. He started jumping up and down very excitedly because he knew the girls would get in big trouble if caught in the rain barrel. Of course, he did not tell them their parents were coming. When the parents were on the porch, he started describing what the girls were doing and laughing. The parents were furious. I don't think I have to tell you what happened next. There was running, crying, spanking, hiding, and pleading for mercy. The girls got whipped and told never to do that again. Their job was to empty the rain barrel and add fresh water from the well until the rain again filled it up.

My mother was in the next room as he told me the story, and somehow there were minor differences between her version of the story to the one he told. I love my mother, but I liked his version. (smile)

Curtain Stretching

In the fall, trees prepare to rest for the cold winter. The leaves change many beautiful hues before shedding: red, orange, yellow, and brown, then fall one by one to the ground. Laying on the ground, they become dry and brittle, crunching as you walk. (What do you do with all the fallen leaves, you ask? That's a story for another day.)

The air is less humid. Days are shorter and a little more relaxed. Families have returned home from much-needed and enjoyed vacations. School will soon start following the summer break. Kids are anxious to return to school and see old friends and new teachers. Mom's can't wait either. It's time to put summer behind us and get busy getting everything ready to settle in for the long winter months that will be here before you know it. I firmly believe adults stay up nights dreaming up things for the kids to do to assist with this transition. Kids in their right mind never liked these arduous monumental annual jobs. I was one of them.

Moms were always good at finding jobs to do for seasonal change. Of all the jobs that needed to be done, my least favorite was Curtain Stretching. This was a big production, and mom led the charge. If you were born before the Civil Rights era, you probably know what I am talking about. Otherwise, you are wondering what this is all about. Let me explain.

Screens had to be changed, and window treatments had to be taken down, washed, and put away. Screens were changed to storm windows which kept out more of the cold weather. Sheer or lace curtains were replaced with lined drapes for the same reason. When the curtains were taken down and washed, mom would starch them to guarantee a certain crispness when they dried. Enough starch was added to the curtains so they could virtually stand up unassisted.

A conglomerate of wooden rails were put together to form an adjustable rectangular frame standing independently on four legs. Each rail had nails from end to end jutting out every 1/2 inch. I can almost hear mom saying, "be careful not to stick your fingers." The nails were sharp, thin, and half the length of a straight pin. From a child's perspective, this thing looked a little monstrous.

To stretch the curtain, first, you would take the washed and starched curtain, soaking wet, dripping with starch, and along every edge of the frame, attach the edge of the curtain to the pins on the frame at 1/2 inch intervals starting from the top to the bottom. This would help keep the curtain from touching or dragging on the floor as you complete all four sides. My fingers would get pierced, and out came an "ouch." All ten fingers would be damaged when all the curtains were hung on the frame. You would layer each panel one on top of the other to get all the panels hung for one drying session. I never thought my fingers would work well for anything ever again, especially playing the piano at my lessons on Saturdays.

This was a tedious job, and who knows how many finger pricks you had by the time you were done. Mom put a rug or plastic covering on the floor to catch any possible drips. You did not want to get any starchy liquid on her hardwood floors.

As soon as all four sides of the curtain were attached to the frame, you would adjust and lock the frame's height and width to make the curtain taut. At this point, it was stretched tight with no excess or wrinkles. You could bounce a coin off the curtain. It was that tight. The curtains remained on the stretcher for at least 24 hours or until they were completely dry.

Once the curtains dried, they could virtually stand up on their own because of the amount of starch in them. They were crisp and beautiful. Two people would hold a round tube the width of the curtain to begin carefully rolling the curtain onto the tube, not allowing one wrinkle. More than one curtain panel could be rolled on each tube. Finally, the tube was wrapped from one end to the other with a sheet or plastic covering to protect the curtains while in storage through the winter.

The Curtain Stretching was a long, arduous task repeated for each window's curtains. Each window in the house had two panels of curtains. Mom had several frames and could do more than one curtain at a time on each frame.

Next spring, mom would remove the heavy lined drapes, wash the windows, pull the rollers out of storage, un-roll them, and put those beautifully starched curtains back on the clean windows. Seeing how beautiful they looked, just looking at them made all that work worthwhile. Later, the drapes would be washed and put away without any particular process.

Did I mention that this was my least favorite fall job? My mom made it seem fun helping her. She always made freshly baked cookies to go along with the work. Mom always made complex tasks "taste so good."

Let me think About It...

Mom knew that the answer might be no, at any given time, but she would ask anyway. I was expected to respond favorably to each request. Often my response was, "let me think about it." Not wanting to say no to her request. She would tell me that she already knew that whenever I said that, the answer would always be no. I would say, "well, do you want me to say no now or no later?" We would laugh about that. Sometimes, mom would spend time considering "to-do's" that I probably did not have time "to-do" or have any interest in doing. She wanted to complete the items on her "to-do" list while I was back in town. Her list would take up what little time I had between work trips. There were many balls in the air, and I did what I could to keep them up there, allowing none to fall. In other words, keeping everyone happy with little time, was hard.

Years later, my daughter often reminded me that she was called to take mom to get her a Junior Bacon Cheeseburger from her favorite restaurant. Mom would say, "I just want to get a JBC, and she doesn't have time. Would you take me?" thank goodness for my daughter stepping in. My daughter always said yes. I was grateful for her caring for mom when I had no more hours in my day.

Mile High

In Denver, the Broncos football game is the biggest thing going on game day. Even at church, people going to the game would have part of their game garb on so they would be ready to dash out as soon as the benediction was given. Season ticket holders always kept their spots. They were hard to come by. The waiting list was at that time about twenty years. I got a blessing from one of my customers that had tickets, and the family was leaving the state and wanted to sell their season passes. What a break. If they had just let them go and not paid to renew their season tickets, they would have been sold by the stadium to the next person on that twenty-year waiting list.

I called my husband, telling him about the availability of some coveted season tickets, and we both agreed immediately to get the tickets. We had season tickets for a few years. I asked my mother if she would like to go to one of the preseason games in August when it wasn't cold, and my husband would not have a problem not going to the game since it was a preseason game. Mom said, "yes." She knew nothing about football, nor had she ever been to a football game. One thing I loved about mom is that she was always willing and ready to try new things.

When we arrived at Mile High Stadium, we got snacks, so we did not have to get up later. I knew where our seats were because, with season tickets, you always had the same seats.

We got to our seats, and I knew and spoke to everybody near us because people in your section are like family. They were always the same. Getting there early was good, so my mom could take her time. I explained everything to her while we waited for the game to begin. The sun was intense, and it was late afternoon. Mom brought an umbrella to shade her from the sun. That was ok for now, but I explained that we would cause a riot if she tried to put up an umbrella during the game, which would, in essence, block the view of some behind her. Since our section was like family, I would not tick them off, knowing I would see those same people at the next game.

Mom was unhappy about closing the umbrella when the game started because the sun was still intense. After all, we are talking about the Mile High City. There, it's all about the sun and how close it is to us. We survived the game. She enjoyed her outing but probably couldn't tell you about any plays made that day or the score.

Out to Lunch

Going out to lunch is usually about more than just eating. My mom, cousin, a friend, and I went out to lunch, enjoying ourselves for hours. It did not seem like a long time; we laughed and enjoyed ourselves. When we returned home many hours later, my brother Jack, asked where we had been all day. "At lunch" was the simultaneous response. He laughed as though he didn't believe us, "it doesn't take that long to eat," he said. I explained that eating lunch with your "people" is not just about eating lunch. It's the fellowship and conversation (Koinonia). We get caught up on each other's lives and families. I can't tell you how guys catch up with each other because I am not a guy. Maybe that's what's wrong with them. They need to "catch up" and not hold so much inside, calling it "ego." Koinonia might simply be a woman thing.

I miss those extraordinary times with the ladies. Upon moving to a different state, the dynamics are not the same. First, I need to establish those deep relationships. Second, the culture is so different, not diverse, just different. Many are homebodies, some don't like to drive at night, and others don't want to eat out. If they eat out, we go where oatmeal is on the menu. Yuck. There are many different cuisines available, and often I find myself going and eating alone. I like myself and am comfortable alone, but it's not Koinonia. You can have food alone but not fellowship or Koinonia alone.

Aunt Sugar

My brother Othello, we called him Junior, would come and take me out to practice driving so I could get my license when I turned sixteen. He was a patient teacher and never seemed to be frightened at my learning to drive. We went out every weekend until I could take my road test for my license. Later, living in Brooklyn, he connected me with Aunt Sugar (my dad's sister), that lived near me. We had never met, but my mother knew her from years prior. Eventually, my mom and I went to see Aunt Sugar. Realizing we lived less than two miles from each other, we started doing many things together in New York.

Aunt Sugar and my mom both liked to go to the horse race track. We went at least once a year after that. Eventually, my mom moved into an apartment in the same building where Aunt Sugar lived. They constantly came up with places to go and things to do. Neither of them drove, so I did all the driving. Tai-Tanisha was small and hung out with us all the time. There was shopping and other activities too.

I was so glad my brother got us connected. Unfortunately, not many years later, he passed away, and I miss him. Thankfully, we had a chance to make this connection, and I was able to share with him, the activities we did with Aunt Sugar before he passed.

One year my daughter and I went to Trinidad and Tobago for a vacation. On our return trip, we made plans to stop in Georgia and meet one of my cousins, Ulysses. Aunt Sugar introduced me to him over the phone before we left for Trinidad. We spent a week with him. He took us to meet other family members. Ulysses was a schoolteacher and lived in the country on a farm.

Monticello is a very small town with few sightseeing attractions, but he showed us the school where he worked, the courthouse where my mom and dad got married, the house they lived in, and some family homes. He lived in the country outside the main section of town with no street lights, air-conditioning, or indoor plumbing. This was his parents' home and where he grew up. Becoming a teacher and an assistant principal, Ulysses could easily afford to live where there were more conveniences but chose to live and farm on the property that belonged to his family.

There was a cow, some chickens, and a few other creatures in his yard. Tai-Tanisha was a preschooler and had never seen a real cow. Playing outside in her bare feet, she walked up to see the cow that was fenced in and got a little freaked out. Running in her bare feet to the back door and screaming, "Mom, come see the monster in the back yard." I could not imagine what she was talking about, but I quickly got some shoes on and ran out to see the monster. To my surprise and elation, it was only a cow. Explaining to Tai-Tanisha about the cow and what the cow provides for us in our diet and assuring her that the cow was not a monster, she calmed down and was no longer afraid. We lived in Brooklyn, and there were no cows in the yards. This was a new phenomenon for her.

This was all new to my daughter and me. Going out in the backyard to the potty was challenging during the day. Yes, there were spiders and no lights in the outdoor facility. In the dark of night was not something I was going to do. Planning was essential; we made sure all was done before dark. Bathing was in a tub sitting in the middle of the kitchen. Having only read about the history of a time gone by came to life for me on that trip. Eventually, we would return to Brooklyn and could get a shower and go to the restroom indoors at any time of the day or night. However, I am thankful I had an opportunity to experience what I had only read about. This journey increased my understanding of what older generations went through and gave me a greater appreciation for what I take for granted.

Aunt Sugar had told us about all of my cousins in Georgia, but we had not met them. I remember her telling me about my cousin Ida, who was about my age, and that we had many similarities, which made me want to meet her. However, on that trip, she was not to be found. I didn't catch up with her until years later. Now, Ida and I are more than cousins; she is like the sister I never had. Her sister Lois and I have also grown very close to each other. I love those ladies. God has put these ladies in my life for "such a time as this."

Years later, Aunt Sugar retired, moved back to Georgia from Brooklyn, and we moved to Colorado. We would fly down to visit her and once again spend time in the country. She lived in a different country town. She had lights, indoor plumbing, and bathroom facilities, which was a different experience.

Ida is one to stay on the phone for only a short time, maybe only "five minutes", that might be what she and Jeff have in common. But my cousin Lois and I can stay on the phone longer. Still, that doesn't come close to challenging my cousin Jeff's calls from New Orleans. Lois likes politics and is my political guru, and we have lots to discuss. If I miss a news story, she can update me. I think the world of Ida and Lois and wish we had grown up together. We only met as adults. I wonder what exciting things we could have shared if Lois, Ida, Viola, and I had known each other all of our lives. We have never missed a beat since we got acquainted. We have traveled together and shared with other family members. My mom loved them and looked forward to traveling to the annual Thanksgiving family dinner in Atlanta each year.

On the Way to LA

I prefer to travel any way except on a bus. But mom didn't mind the bus. The year my youngest grandson was due to be born, I was on a work assignment and unable to go to be with my daughter and her family in Louisiana. My assistant, mom, decided she wanted to go and be there for the new arrival. Mom had recently celebrated her ninetieth birthday. She was in good health and sound mind. She could not have been more ready and able to make this journey. The bus was the best option for her. I wasn't thrilled because she had to make different connections two or three times from Pittsburgh to get there. She did not have a cell phone to communicate with me during her trip, they were just becoming popular.

I gave her specific written details of where to change busses, the bus numbers, and to notice where the bus said it was headed. She needed to know how long each layover was and what to look for at each station. We made sure she had snacks with her and emphasized the importance of safety by sitting in the front seat and not leaving any valuables in the seat if you were stopping for a potty break. I almost forgot, "the arrival and departure times from each station stop will differ from what your watch says because you are changing time zones." On her note with her detailed instructions, I included the time her watch says and the actual time at the city where she was arriving. I gave her the exact change for the payphones and instructions to call me at every stop. She did well at that.

The trip is about a twenty-hour journey, including layovers between bus schedules. "Don't talk to strangers." I don't know why I even bothered to say that because before she arrived at her destination, she would know everybody by name, why they were traveling, and probably when they would return. She never listened to me about stranger danger.

My daughter, Tai-Tanisha, was clocking everything from her end. She knew exactly when she was to arrive, taking into consideration the time zone change. I had to write a book for the passenger and the pickup person.

Don't forget that the purpose of the trip was to be there for the arrival of Tai-Tanisha's child. Shortly after mom arrived safely at my daughter's, only a day or two passed before she went into the hospital to deliver her child. Soon I got a call at my business conference that the baby was here, "it's a boy," Michael II. Mom was excited and glad she was there to help with the baby and the other children during this time. The bus trip was long and arduous but worth it. In a few weeks, she will have to make the return trip. No worries, she is a pro at this traveling thing now. She will be fine.

Caught at the Bus Stop

$\mathcal{E}$ach morning I would head straight to the highway and directly to work. I was a creature of habit and rarely deviated from my route. Boring! After allowing a little extra time to go to the post office to drop off my bill payment, I took a slightly different route one morning. The route included turning right to the post office and then a bee-line to the highway and my office.

Today, I took a shortcut near the senior citizen's high-rise. Speeding along and sipping my coffee, I glanced out my side window to see what appeared to be a stately well-dressed woman standing at the bus stop. It was pretty early in the morning for such a sighting. As I got closer, I kept looking. Either it was a mirage, or the person began to look more and more familiar. After a closer look, I realized it was my mother standing at the bus stop at 7:15 in the morning. Putting on my brakes and pulling over to the curb, I almost spilled my coffee. Rolling down the window on the passenger side and asking, "What are you doing at the bus stop, and where do you think you are going this early in the morning?" Mom asked, "Why are you coming down this street? This isn't the way you go to work?" I followed up with, "Where are you going?" She said, "I am going to visit Mary," her sister-in-law, down in the next county.

Mom would have to take the city bus next to her apartment building to get into town. There would be a four-block walk to the regional bus stop to catch the bus that goes to the next county where her sister-in-law lived. This time of morning creates yet another problem, it's right in the midst of rush hour, and plenty of workers, students, and early shoppers would be headed downtown. She stood confident and had the exact money in her hand for the bus ride, and it was only a minute or so before the bus arrived. She knew the schedule. Obviously, this was not her first "pony ride." She had done this before.

Insisting that she get in my car, mom reluctantly got in, looking a little sheepish because she got caught. I dropped my bill in the post office mailbox and headed straight to my Aunt Mary's house to drop off my mother. I tried to insist that she not try this again, encouraging her to call me, and I would take her where she wanted to go. She didn't want to bother me since I was always so busy. That was not the reason; she just wanted to be "grown."

We laughed about that morning and how she insisted that she was "grown" and did not have to tell me when and where she was going. I harped on the fact that she was 93 years old and could have the decency to let me know where she was going, especially since it was quite a journey, unlike going across the street to the market. We bantered and laughed all the way to Aunt Mary's house, about forty-five minutes away. We said so long, and I told her when I would pick her up later that evening. She nodded in agreement as we both shook our heads for different reasons.

Later, I picked her up and took her home. When she got out of the car, we said good night as she turned to enter her building. We both knew this was not her last time sneaking out alone. Nevertheless, whenever I think about that day, I can't help but smile and wonder how many other times she got away with something like this. Knowing her, she moved her schedule to ensure I had gone to work before leaving and standing at the bus stop.

In today's world, mom would be safe from getting caught because bill paying, by most people, is done online when due or set up with each biller to be withdrawn automatically from your account on its arranged date. No need to go to the post office to mail the payment or to the company and stand in line to pay. If I had not been going to the post office to send my bill, she would not have gotten caught, and she would have been safe being "GROWN."

Roadrunner

Never staying still and traveling must be part of a person's DNA. Some people seem too afraid to go downtown. Some don't want to go out at night. Never ask some people about going out of town. Those are not characteristics of my mom and this family. We can't seem to stay still. Going to Washington, D.C. had been planned for a while. The bi-annual family reunion in Chicago happened to fall at the same time this year. It was a toss-up, go to the reunion or to go on my trip. Mom decided to go to the reunion and ride there with a nephew. My daughter, her children, and I chose not to go to the reunion this year but instead to D.C.

The day the reunion ended, we were leaving for our D.C. trip. Because we forgot something and doubled back to get it, we had a later start than planned. As we were driving down the turnpike, minding our business, I looked out the driver's side window; who do I see but my mom riding in the car with her nephew, returning from Chicago. She recognized us and started frantically waving to get our attention. There was no cell phone to call each other. We waited for an opportune time to pull over safely. She asked, "where are you guys going?" Explaining that we were headed to D.C., she decided that instead of going home, she would come with us. Mom and her luggage left one car, and she got in with us on the Pennsylvania Turnpike.

What is the chance of seeing someone you know as you are speeding along on the turnpike? Even if we had been intentionally trying to catch up with someone, the likelihood of that would have been slim to none. When we got to Gwen's house in D.C., we explained the story, and no one could believe it. They thought it was hilarious. We had a great time with Gwen and her dad. Mom has since been affectionately known as the "Roadrunner."

My job asked if I would go to Paris and Brazil pretty close to the end of my career, spending six months in each place. I chose not to go because my mom, even though she was healthy, did not want to make another move. Funny, since all her life she was always willing to explore new things and was comfortable traveling everywhere. I was surprised she did not want to go. Although my daughter wanted to go. I turned down the offer because I was not going that far without mom especially since she was in her nineties. If I had asked her one more time, she would have gone, no doubt about it. Looking back now, Paris may not be part of my bucket list, it may have been considered HOME.

PART 7

Family/House

Do your best to present yourself to God as one approved, a worker who does not need to be ashamed and who correctly handles the word of truth.

2 Timothy 2:15 NIV

Eastern Place

Growing up in a home that is considered multi-generational has many memories. There were three generations there. Several second-generation members came and went in and out of the house over the years. I moved in five days after being born at Herman Keifer hospital. Various roomers lived in apartments in the basement from time to time. They were not related to us.

How all the people who lived there did so without confusion baffles me. Eventually, Grandma Emma and Grandpa Kelly moved out as well as Aunt Bea and Uncle Lee. Grandma Emma and Grandpa Kelly moved into an apartment only a block and a half away. Aunt Bea and Uncle Lee were across town.

The basement was where the coal furnace lived. The fruit cellar was where my grandma kept the food she canned. In the winter, someone had to stoke the fire, add more coal when needed, and clean out the ashes. The boys usually did that. Thank goodness I was not old enough to do that job. I stayed as far away from the furnace as possible. The basement was scary; I wouldn't say I liked it. I went to the basement to be with my mother when she did the laundry. It was always interesting since we had a wringer washing machine and no dryer. Had they been invented yet? I do not think so. We hung clothes on the lines in the basement and outside when the weather permitted. Grandpa Kelly used the basement to make his moonshine to sell. It became imperative for him and Grandma Emma to move so the house would not be in jeopardy of confiscation if it were found that illegal practices were being performed.

Behind the kitchen and the upstairs bathroom was an addition that was added to the house. All the boys slept there, Robert and Jack, slept in the upstairs room and Melvin and James slept in the downstairs room. The only way to access Robert and Jacks's room was through the bathroom. Once, I remember them having some friends in their room. I was taking a bath, and they all came passing through the bathroom while I was bathing. How embarrassing. However, I was only a little kid, about three years old. They didn't care, but I did.

Swimming

I always heard that Melvin was a good swimmer and had received many accolades. I did not know that he developed his love of swimming after a near-miss accident. He almost drowned at the McMichael pool. He and some friends were chasing each other, and he jumped in to get away from them, not knowing he was jumping into the deep end. Melvin could not swim. He did not even know there was a deep and shallow end. He would have drowned if the lifeguard had not been quick. He was only ten years old.

After that, he would not go swimming for a long time. He sat on the porch steps each day as his friends passed by on their way to the swimming pool, he got tired of missing all the summer fun. He soon got enough courage to take lessons and return to the pool. After much hard work and his eventual love for swimming, in 1952, he received the Bronze medal for swimming competitions at the recreational center.

Hoopty

We were raised to get an after-school or weekend job to save for the things we wanted to buy. Times were tough, and we needed to realize that items did not appear without earning them. My cousin Melvin had a paper route and a whopping one hundred eighty-nine customers. His paper route and his job at Western Union delivering telegrams on his bicycle allowed him to save for his car.

Our grandparents and parents never learned to drive. The next generation considered it a big deal to have a car. We shuttled them everywhere they wanted to go and ran errands for neighbors and others when needed. All the boys wanted cars to entice the girls to see how "cool" they were and get them to go for a ride.

Usually, that first car was different from the ones we saw in a commercial or on the magazine cover. Often, it falls in the category of what we call a "Hoopty." To state it mildly, it needed some work done on it. However, it still made it down the block and to the filling station (now known as the gas station).

Almost everyone reading this story would agree that only one out of ten people have ever heard of a 1949 Kaiser Frazer. He was 18 when he bought this car. It did not look like a "Hoopty." It was well put together. Imagine that. In 1956 the price he paid for the vehicle was one hundred dollars. Gas was eighteen cents per gallon.

You hear stories and see older television shows where guys took their dates to drive-in theaters (most of you have never been to one of these). The guys liked going to the drive-in because it was like going to "lovers lane." Probably much hanky panky went on in those cars parked in the drive-in. There was also a "lovers lane" in Belle Isle park. (Belle Isle was an island park with fishing, swimming, barbecuing, a kid's zoo, and various hangout areas.) However, there were no movies to see at the park. It's been twenty or thirty years since drive-in theaters were famous. Although, there is one still operating about a half hour from my home today.

Once Melvin had transportation, he acquired lots of friends. Everybody did not have a car, but those who did became quite popular. Melvin drove his car everywhere. They went to the Greystone ballroom on the weekends to dance. The Greystone was everything. If you thought you were cool, you had to be there. Many of the Motown stars and other famous singers went there regularly. As the driver, he and his friends went to Toledo, Ohio, to roller skate weekly. I overheard on several occasions that he got speeding tickets going back and forth to Toledo to skate. He shouldn't have been going so fast in that huge car.

Graduate

No one in the family had ever graduated from high school until Melvin in 1957. He was excited and rushed to get ready, so he would not be late for the graduation. It was indeed a big deal. Aunt Emma, his mom, was too slow and wasn't getting ready fast enough. She did not make it to the graduation ceremony. However, grandma saw his excitement and decided she would not miss this historic occasion for anything. She quickly got ready and left with Melvin. They hurried to catch the bus to the event. She was so proud to see him be the first person in our family to graduate, walk across that stage, and receive his diploma.

After graduation, he dated and married Ernestine and later had two children, Sophia and Terrance. A great opportunity came for them to relocate to Los Angeles, California. Never having experienced an earthquake, once the first set of tremors hit, they were ready to return to Detroit, and they did.

Cars Cars Cars

The 1949 Ford V8 convertible, his "Hot Rod," was so cool that even my grandfather Kelly employed him to drive some items to Beaver County, Pennsylvania. When they arrived, Melvin learned that they were transporting homemade whiskey. Uncle Buster lived in a dry county and sold whiskey out of his home, either pints or shots. There were better ways, I believe, that Melvin could use his time and car.

Detroit did not hold his attention for long. He was itching for something more. California did not work out, but there must be something else. Some time passed, and an opportunity came for him and his family to move to New York. They lived there for quite a while, and he seemed to thrive in New York. He had a couple more children there, Melvin, and Tashia. I don't know what kind of hold Detroit had on him, but after a long time, once again, he returned home to Detroit to live.

Melvin came home driving a 1961 Chrysler New Yorker Deluxe. We called it his Batmobile. It resembled the car used on the TV show Batman. It was convertible and sleek, not bulky like the Kaiser Frazer. Occasionally, I got a ride in it. I wished I could drive it, but I was not quite old enough yet. Knowing how much he liked that car, I don't think he would let anyone, much less me, drive that car.

It wasn't until 1969, at twenty-nine years old, Melvin traded in his Batmobile and purchased his first new car. This time he got a brand new Chrysler 300, gold, for three thousand dollars.

Melvin later met and married Shirley Ann. They are still together today. I always admired him because he was the first person in the family to be a high school graduate; he chose to embrace life by exploring new things, like moving to California and then to New York. I thought that was cool and took courage. No one in our family had experienced anything like that; we are proud of him. I looked up to him as a brother, not just a cousin.

I have done a sufficient amount of research on our family tree. We lived and grew up in the same house, were raised by the same people, experienced the same things, and ate the same food. Whenever I asked him a question about something back then, most of the time, his answer to my question was, "I have no idea." There are probably some things that could have been added to this narrative, but I think he has "selective memory." When I try to clarify some fact, he always, without hesitation, says either, "I have no idea" or "C.R.S." (Can't Remember s.h.i.t.)

Only Five Minutes

After my family migrated from the south, some only wanted to return for a visit, others not at all. My grandparents went twice, and my mom, aunts, my husband, and I went once. I saw where my mom grew up and lived, specific landmarks, jobs, and schools. My visit encouraged me to become interested in family history and genealogy.

When I was about eight years old, I asked grandma where she was born, who her parents were, and if she had any sisters and brothers. Years later, I asked my grandpa the same questions. Believe it or not, I got lots of information that I wrote down and filed away somewhere.

As an adult, I became very interested in genealogy and pulled out all the information I had gotten from my grandmother and grandfather. I combined their input with my research and published a book about my grandmother's family. It opened my eyes to events from slavery in the south until now that I knew little about. My book is titled *From The Rising of The Sun....* I began researching my Grandpa Kelly's family, the McCoys and the Pattersons, only a few years ago. I uncovered information online that connected me to a cousin with much more research experience in this area than I had.

Jeff and I struck up a relationship, and I have learned so much from him and his family tree, which includes all of my family. Jeff has assisted me in expanding my tree on the Patterson side to have over a thousand people listed. It is still and will probably be a forever work in progress. He has taken me back much farther than I could have gone on my own. He is a funny guy. I have tried to limit our calls to five minutes since he nor I know how to get off the phone. When I call now, I immediately say, "only five minutes." He laughs because we will eventually hang up in four to five hours. I want to give a shout-out to his wife, Sandra, for loaning him to me for genealogy purposes.

We laugh a lot from trying to get me up to speed on Ancestry family tree knowledge. Jeff shakes his head as he repeats something to me more than once. Now he has an advocate, my cousin Ida, who tends to side with him on everything against me. He also threatens to call my daughter Tai-Tanisha if I am acting up. All of this is good fun for us all. Jeff was also instrumental in introducing me to Estella, another of my cousins on the Patterson line. She has been such a joy to get to know and was bubbling over with enthusiasm at meeting me.

Estella had never met any offspring from Peter Patterson, our great-grandfather, other than her siblings. We have begun to talk more, but not as much as Jeff and I, but I am looking forward to a time when we all will meet face to face. We have plans to go to a family reunion next summer, where we will finally see each other. Go Pattersons! Jeff is very managerial, fun to talk to, and seems to be an expert on just about everything. He holds a fantastic amount of knowledge about genealogy. I will never be able to catch him, nor will I try. I sometimes get no love. (smile) The lesson learned is never to call Jeff if you only have five minutes to talk. Estella and I enjoy our talks and especially the ones where we are talking about Jeff.

Don't Touch that Baby

Aunt Bea's son Robert was one of my cousins who lived upstairs in the bedroom behind the bathroom. I had not seen him for a while and was unsure what had happened to him. Mom told me he had been drafted by the army and served overseas in Korea. A war was going on.

After serving in the army, he married and moved into the basement with Joy, his new wife. Sounds coming from the basement had me trying to figure out what else was down there. Being only four years old, I was too afraid to go down there and see. I only went in the basement with mom when she did the laundry. Asking mom about the sounds, she explained that a baby was in the basement with Robert and Joy. A baby, and it was a girl. I was so excited.

Sometimes I could hear the baby crying when I was upstairs in the kitchen. I could not figure out where the baby came from. Time after time, I tried to sneak down the basement stairs, occasionally making it partway, to see this new baby named Roberta. I was too afraid to go all the way down. I could not see her from the stairs. Sometimes I would stand in the kitchen at the basement door, listening to sounds of moving around coming from the basement.

One day, when the baby woke up, Joy brought her upstairs and laid her on the couch. I was overjoyed, jumping up and down, happy to see the baby. Her mom always said, "Don't touch the baby. Just look."

My answer was always, "Ok," but that was not what I wanted to say or meant. When mom was home, she would hold the baby and have me sit nicely beside her so I could hold the baby with her assistance. "Hold her nicely, so we don't drop her," mom would say. Those little fingers and arms were so cute. I would smile and talk to her, but she never did say anything back. She always looked at me as if she could understand what I was saying to her. She liked me too.

Cooking, talking, and hanging up clothes outside to dry were always happening at our home. As the baby grew, they would ask me to watch her as she was lying on the couch while her mom hung clothes on the line to dry in the backyard. Usually, she was asleep when I watched her. I was glad to have this job. I watched closely to ensure that nothing happened to Roberta; I really liked her. I was a good watcher. When she was awake, Roberta watched me. Her eyes followed me as I moved around. She made strange sounds as she tried to talk in what seemed like another language. I did not understand a word of it. We laughed, but I do not believe we were laughing at the same thing.

Every day I looked forward to watching the baby, and I waited in the kitchen, at the top of the basement stairs for her mom to bring her up. When she did, I was ready for my assignment. I think we both were. One day when she was lying on the couch, the doorbell rang, and Roberta's mom went to see who was there, saying to me, "Don't touch the baby." I don't know who was at the door, but they stood talking for a while. Roberta started whimpering, so I sat down next to her, reached over, remembering what I saw everyone else do, and picked her up and put her nicely on my lap. Sitting very still and smiling, making sure not to drop her, everything seemed fine. She stopped whimpering.

I did not hear the front door close or hear her mom come back into the room to check on her. Entering the room, Joy saw me holding the baby. She threw up her hands as her eyes got big before she screamed,

"What are you doing? You are not to touch the baby." Frightened, I jumped up from the couch with the baby on my lap and as I did Roberta fell crashing to the floor. She started screaming, and I started crying because I was afraid. Her mom yelled at me for touching Roberta. She picked the baby up from the floor and began to rub her and wipe her tears. I ran upstairs crying and sat on the top step. I could hear someone calling my name, but I did not answer or come down. I was never going to come down again. Was Roberta all right?

Soon grandma came looking for me and sat on the step beside me. I had stopped crying by then. She asked if I was "Ok." I did not say anything. She hugged me and said softly, "Roberta is all right." I smiled. That took care of Roberta. What about me? I was not supposed to touch her. I did what I saw everyone else do, she sat nicely on my lap, and there was no problem. I did it right. Roberta liked it, too. "She stopped whimpering. Didn't her mom notice that when she walked into the room? Why did she scream at me?" I asked. Grandma explained, "Babies are so gentle, and sometimes children do not know how to handle them. Even though you were sitting nicely, it frightened Roberta's mom; she didn't mean it."

Furthermore, grandma said, " As long as you are ok, that's all I care about. "I love you, grandma," I said and gave her a big hug. "Let's go down and tell her mom that you are sorry for dropping the baby because when she screamed at you, it frightened you." "I was taking care of her," I said. "Let's tell her how much you love the baby and like watching her. She will understand," said grandma. I did not get punished. That was just fine with me. However, I was still sad because I made the baby cry and got yelled at.

Her mom never held that against me. We always got along fine. As I grew and two other children came along, her mom became less protective of her children or more trusting of me. You know how it is with the first baby, and sometimes moms let their guard down a little when the second child arrives, realizing that they are not as breakable as they once thought, first Ricky and later Rowland.

Even after becoming an adult, we would laugh hard about this when it came up. Roberta and I have always been close, and even though she can be a little 'wacky,' we sometimes, jokingly, blame it on the fall. We all have joked about that throughout the years. Families remember the best stories and lovingly laugh at them. This is one of those stories that never goes away. With truth, it is what it is. Love you, Roberta.

White Castle

I can remember helping Aunt Bea with errands and bill paying. She would drive up to a building, and Roberta or I would jump out, run to pay the bill and get back to the car. We saved her from having to find and possibly pay for parking just to run in and pay a bill. Our reward would be to eat out. There were no fast food restaurants as we know them today during those days. Only White Tower and White Castle. We loved White Castle the best. Believe it or not, they are still around, and I go there when I visit Michigan. Every location has long lines and is open 24/7.

We are just some of the ones who liked them. You could tell by the long lines for ordering. When Aunt Bea treated Roberta and me, we could get as many hamburgers as we wanted. They were small, about two square inches, and cost only twelve cents each. One day Roberta challenged me to see who could eat the most hamburgers. She was always trying to beat me. She thought she could. Being older, I thought I could beat her and took the challenge. We each ordered fifteen hamburgers and a drink. We went at it. It was a race. Suddenly I slowed down, asking her how many she had eaten. Roberta said, "I am up to ten." I had only eaten eight. I was about to stall out. She went on and finished twelve, beating me by about four hamburgers. Someone was sick the next day, me. If you have never had a White Castle hamburger, you do not know what you are missing. They are small juicy, and flavorful. Today those same-sized twelve-cent hamburgers cost more than seventy-five cents and taste just as good or better.

My first car could have been called a "Hoopty." It certainly needed some work but it did the job of getting me from point A to point B. After getting my driver's license, I was charged with taking Roberta, Ricky, Rowland, Valerie, and Roslyn, everywhere. I was expected to take Valerie and Roslyn to Gethsemane School, everybody to church, and whoever needed to go to the grocery store. I was glad to have a car of my own at sixteen to go anywhere. They thought I was their chauffeur. I did not care because it gave me a chance to drive and some freedom in my responsibilities.

Over the years, Roberta, her brothers, Ricky and Rowland, and I remain incredibly close. We talk regularly even now. Maybe not Ricky so much; it is sometimes hard to catch up with him. We call each other and talk when I can find him. Early this year, we were together, unfortunately, for their dad, Robert's funeral. He and his wife, Christine, were victims of a house fire. Rest in peace, Robert and Christine.

It's A Party

$\mathcal{D}$o you remember trying to make a call when there were only party lines? What about regular rotary dial phones that were not modular, meaning they were permanently attached to the wall? I am sure you don't remember unless you are "as old as dirt" like me.

When I was a child, there were no portable wall jacks or cordless phones. Most people had a "party line" service. With that service, you had your own phone number but had to share the lines outside the home that ran through the street. If you picked up your phone to make a call, someone who lived in a different house could be talking. You had to wait until they were done to get a free line to make your call. That could be hours. You could yell at them and try to get them to hurry.

However, if they wanted to be a butt, they could hold you up, even laying their phone down with an open line for as long as they wanted, and there was nothing you could do about it. You could also stay on and listen to their conversation or keep interrupting. It was a good idea to be friendly with the people on your "party line."

Different types of party lines existed; there were two-party, four-party, and six-party line services. What you paid for determined how many households were on your party line service. The less you paid for your service, the more families were on your party line.

Today many homes do not have one phone line. Each family member usually has a cell phone, and house phones are almost non-existent, eliminating even the remote possibility of a "party line" service. Trust me; it was no party.

Chickens

Never send your children to spend time with older relatives who never had children. Your child could be frightened or damaged by the types and preparation of food, sleeping times, and treats. My Grandpa Kelly's sister and her husband, Aunt Margaret and Uncle Zenius, loved me and wanted me to spend part of my summer vacation with them. Our family celebrated many holiday dinners at their home over the years. At first, I thought going to their house was a good idea. I was going on vacation with a packed suitcase. How special.

When I first got to their house, I was ok. I was bored by the end of the first day. No other children were there to play with. I sat around and walked in the garden with Aunt Margaret, who grew many types of vegetables and flowers. She explained what was what and related them to things I was familiar with. Somehow I thought going to Aunt Margaret's, and Uncle Zenius's house would be fun. That was as far from reality as I could have imagined. They were old and never had children, so they did not know what "real" kids liked.

At dinner time, it was evident that the food was not the same as the food at my house, but somehow I managed to eat enough to not be hungry before going to sleep. After dinner, they asked, "would you like some candy?" My eyes lit up, and I said, "yes." My uncle gave me some horehound candy and some licorice. Both were so nasty that I had to spit them out. I did not want anything else they had, even if it sounded familiar. What these older adults call a treat was ultimately quite scary and nasty.

Every morning my mom would prepare different foods for breakfast. Sometimes it was eggs and bacon or sausage. On other days it was cereal, cold or hot. Every weekend mom would make pancakes which were my favorite. When Aunt Margaret asked if I liked oatmeal, I said, "yes." She prepared some for herself and me. We sat and had our breakfast while she asked me many questions about my friends, school, and what I liked doing. My answers were short and quick. I tried the oatmeal that was swimming in milk but did not like it. My mother's oatmeal did not taste like this. I tried and tried to get it to go down my throat, to no avail. Soon Aunt Margaret finished hers as I continued to stir mine. Maybe I thought that if I swirled it around in the milk long enough, it would dissolve or disappear.

My aunt excused herself and went to the basement to do laundry. I sat there staring at the cereal, which seemed like forever. The bathroom was right near me. I thought about how to get rid of the cereal without my aunt finding out. While she was in the basement, I slipped into the bathroom and flushed most of the oatmeal down the toilet. I took my almost empty bowl back to the table and sat in my chair.

When Aunt Margaret returned from the basement, she checked on me to see how I was doing with my breakfast. I told her I was full and did not want anymore. She said, "wow you finished that pretty quickly after stirring it for so long." She even asked me if I had gone to the bathroom; she heard the flush. I told her I had to go badly. I believe she knew I flushed the cereal down the toilet but never said it in words. The rest of the week I was with them, I never had oatmeal again.

On Saturday, we went shopping. The first stop was the poultry market. When we got inside, the smell was awful, and we walked on sawdust that covered the floor. Many cages lined the space on the wall behind the counter where the workers were, each with a chicken inside. Some chickens were brown, some almost red, and some were white. They were all clucking quite loudly. I wondered what we were going to do here.

My aunt asked me which one I liked. Going up and down the row and carefully looking at each chicken, I finally settled on "that one," pointing to the large white chicken. She thought that was a good choice. Aunt Margaret told the worker, pointing to the one I picked, "that one."

The worker opened the cage, took out the chicken, and went into the back room. I thought we were going to take it home like a pet. The next thing I saw was the worker bringing a bag out from the back room. My aunt handed him the money, and he gave her the bag. Both people said thank you, and we left the market. "What happened to the chicken?" I asked my aunt, "did you forget the chicken?" She said, "no, the chicken is in the bag." My eyes opened wide, and probably my mouth too. What had happened to the chicken? She explained, "for us to have the chicken for dinner, they had to prepare it." "You mean, kill it?" I asked. She said, "yes." I did not ask any more questions. That was enough for me to process right there.

Traumatized by the death of the special chicken I had picked, I lost track of everything else that happened that day. I don't know if we stopped anywhere else. The balance of the summer vacation at their home is unremarkable. I couldn't wait for the time to come for me to go home.

Jairo

My brother Jacks's son Jairo was born in Bogata, Colombia, South America, and lived back and forth between there and California until he was ten years old before coming to California to live. His mom Maria and Jairo have been in the states ever since. He attended the Naval Academy, Golden State University, and graduated from an accelerated program at Notre Dame De Namur University in Belmont, California.

Mom and Tai-Tanisha traveled to California to visit her son Jack quite a few years ago. Jairo was very young then, probably in elementary school. Mom had not seen him since he and his mother Maria visited us when he was a toddler in Brooklyn, New York. That was the first time we had met them. There are a few photos to remember that time together. The two children were too young to remember, but when I find the photos I will share them. Mom enjoyed her two grandchildren being together for the first time.

Fast forward, Jairo and his wife Wendy came to see my mom and spent some time with us when we lived in Pittsburgh. That was the first time I saw him since he was a toddler. Both Jairo and Tai-Tanisha were grown and had families of their own. My mom and I picked up Jairo and Wendy from the airport and went out for a good meal to share memories as we got to know each other better.

Jack had not had the opportunity to bring Jairo to visit his grandma and me, so there was a lot to learn. Jairo was somewhat reluctant to come, not knowing what to expect. However, after meeting us he realized we were a warm welcoming family that wanted to reach out and stay in touch from that point on. This time meant a lot since he had not had a chance to spend time with his grandma or me in his youth. We all talked, and Jairo asked mom many questions to get to know her better. She was so pleased to have this opportunity to get to know him. He continued to stay in contact with her for the rest of her life. Actually, I want to thank Wendy for being instrumental in getting this trip to take place.

We visited some of the other relatives he had not met and did some sightseeing around the Three Rivers. Because we are still on opposite coasts, we don't see much of each other, but we stay in contact over the phone.

Wendy has a warm remembrance of my mom teaching them how to cook collard greens, and they cook them that same way even today. They fell in love with them. Mom told them after washing them well to take out the spine, roll, cut, and then cook them with a little bacon grease or seasoned meat. There seems to be a definite connection between food and relationships in this family. Jairo says his dad could find anything in the freezer and put it together for a tasty meal. He was good at that.

I think Jack's cooking style definitely came from my mom and grandma, it was in his blood. There always seemed to be a food connection that went along with deep conversations about history, current events, and life. He had a definite sense of humor that would come out at random times and could catch you off guard if you were not ready for it.

Jairo had many conversations with his dad about the bible and Christianity. He said Jack was a serious believer. A lot of the conversation was from a theological perspective. Jairo says that left him an open path to Jesus. I talked to my brother about spiritual things. When Jack visited me in Pittsburgh he usually always went to church with me as well. Books were very important to Jack, and some of them are still in Jairo's possession. He always wanted to write a book, and Jairo does too. When I was packing to move from Pittsburgh, I found some books Jack left there and sent them to him. He explained to me that books and learning were like gold, very precious. He has always been an avid reader. Reading, writing, and learning are obvious traits in our family, DNA.

I thoroughly enjoy catching up with Jairo when we can, and I hope we get together again soon. I love you, Jairo and Wendy and much love to Maria.

Cousins

Mom was very creative. She could cook and make anything. My cousin Rowland said he thought of her as a chemist of sorts. She would go fishing and come home to cook the fish she caught, and everybody had a good meal. She could make "lye soap" for washing clothes, dishes, and anything else you used soap for. The ingredients were lye and old cooking oil. It came out fantastic, and it worked. Mom told Rowland she was making ice cream and needed to get the salt. He said, "no, it will taste nasty, don't put any salt in the ice cream." She explained how it worked, but he still did not want it. She walked through the back room, with the Hop-Along-Cassidy wallpaper on its walls, to the back door.

When we made ice cream on the weekends, I was the churner. The ice cream maker had to be set up on the back porch. It was not electric. Mom filled the canister with the ice cream mixture, closed it tightly, and put it in the barrel. Next, she poured crushed ice around the canister and packed the top with rock salt. None of the salt could get inside the canister that held the ice cream. Mom would sit me on the back porch steps with the hand churner, and away I would go until it became hard to turn. That's when I knew it was ready.

After removing all evidence of salt from around the rim of the canister, she took it out and opened it carefully. Mom always let us get a spoon to taste the ice cream before she emptied the canister's contents and put the ice cream into the freezer. Rowland got his spoonful of ice cream and realized the salt did not make the ice cream taste bad. He thought it was so good. Rowland learned that the salt helps the ice to freeze, which freezes the canister's contents and does not touch the ice cream itself. Volunteering to do the churning gave you first dibs when taking the "dasher" out of the churn before putting the ice cream in the freezer. There was always a good amount of ice cream stuck to the dasher when mom opened the metal container. Getting the dasher was worth the hard work. Mom was a lady who never took chemistry in school but knew many of its properties.

Olympia

The Harlem Globetrotters basketball team came to the Olympia Stadium in my town every year. It was close to where we lived. Somehow, there was always enough money for us to go and see them. We always had good seats for the game.

We were on a separate row from Aunt Bea. She was about three rows behind us and a little over to the end of the row. She always packed a lunch for us wherever we went. She brought fried chicken which we all loved, a loaf of bread, and something to drink. When it was time for our snacks, she opened the basket with the food, took out some napkins and wrapped the chicken in a slice of bread, handed it to the people in the row ahead of her, and told them to pass it down. She repeated this process until we all had our snacks. I don't know what the man in front of her thought, but we enjoyed our chicken and thought no more about it until we remembered some of the strange things from our childhood, and this was a doozie.

Aunt Bea was one of the original germaphobes. I am surprised she let a stranger come close and handle our food, even if it was in a napkin. Remember, she was the one who wiped down everything, the loaf of bread, the milk container, and anything else, making sure no germs were anywhere near what she was going to eat. Wait a minute. I don't remember her eating any of the "pass done the row chicken," only us. That's right; she was the only one who handled her chicken.

Pick me Up

Aunt Bea was always taking us places since she was the only one with a car and a driver's license. She would pack us in her station wagon with Ricky and Rowland in the third row in the back, sweating and about to faint. She never let us put the windows down. I don't know why. We just learned how to wipe sweat.

When I got my driver's license, many errands fell to me. The adults and kids were glad, and I was too. Many times my duties were to take and pick up kids. Rowland and Ricky said they were so happy when I took them places because all the windows in the car were rolled down, and they loved it. It was still hot, but we had a breeze when the car moved. We couldn't have been happier. It was like we had air-conditioning, but there was none back then. I took them to White Castle for hamburgers, ice cream, the park, and swimming. We had fun in "not my car." Aunt Bea would not have let me drive her car if I wasn't trustworthy.

Suzie

I want to tell you about our pet chicken Suzie. Oh no, not another chicken story. She was a reddish feathered bird. I don't remember where she came from, but she was in the backyard one day. One of the six garages was set up with a perch for her to sleep. She could go in and out of the garage alone; the door stayed partially open. She was trained to come when we called her name. We could shout "Suzie" from the back porch, and she would come running.

Each morning one of us went to the garage to collect one brown egg. We had dried chicken feed and some corn we gave her as treats. Of course, she would peck around in the grass for items she liked. Valerie remembers that when there was no school, it would seem like Suzie would get up earlier and make the cackling sound very loudly so everyone would wake up. That's when everybody wanted to sleep in. Similarly, on school days, Suzie seemed quieter, and you did not hear her.

One day I came home and wanted to make sure Suzie was good for the night, had water, and anything else she needed. I did not see her anywhere. I asked if mom had been out to see about Suzie and both my mom and aunt looked at each other and then back at me, not saying a word. Valerie and Roslyn came running to tell me what had happened earlier. They told me my mom and Uncle Irving had been in the basement swinging Suzie by the neck, and Uncle Irving was waiting to finish her off and clean everything up. Valerie said, "we ran back up the stairs and shut the door screaming, they are in the basement killing Suzie." They were scared.

That night there was chicken for dinner. I did not eat any. Oh no, I was not going to eat Suzie, she was our pet, and you don't eat your pets. I strangely did not feel the same about the brown egg each day.

Jasmine

Have you heard the phrase that laughter is like medicine for the soul? My soul must be healthy because my niece Jasmine (my brother Jack's daughter) and I laugh a lot whenever we talk. There is always something interesting that causes us to give a couple of good loud laughs.

We always find a way to get "salad" into the conversation. The first time she came to Pittsburgh to visit us, we shared some of each of our favorite things. Salad was one of them. Let me explain. When she and her brother Emil would come home from school, sometimes they got dinner started for their mom. When Nini got home things were well on their way. Nini always insisted on having a salad at the end of each meal. Her phrase was, "there is always room for salad." My family always begins our meals with salad, not end with it. I thought that a little odd when I first heard it. However, it is always good to learn new cultural traditions. My family had more cooked vegetables than salads, and she loved the collard greens my mom made.

Before I retired from my communications career, I had an opportunity to work and design a system cutover in one of our California offices. I stayed at the Doubletree Hotel in Anaheim. While I was there, Jasmine came down to the Los Angeles area and spent a couple of days with me. We had a lot of fun and saw a few interesting things. She showed me Venice Beach. We walked the beach boardwalk and engaged in the shops and diners there. I even liked watching the young men play basketball and lift weights on the beach in the sand. I had never seen that sport on a beach.

On the boardwalk were people dressed in various styles, some a little risqué and others somewhat wild and crazy. It was truly eclectic. There were a plethora of normal and unusual things and places to see. We popped into a shop that had a sign about tattoos and piercings. After having a conversation with Jasmine about some of the things I would see in the shop, I just had to go in and ask questions. I did not believe her. She went in with me, and the shop owner said he was busy and for us to just look through some of the catalog books on the counter to get an idea of what I wanted. Opening the book and beginning to turn some of the pages, my mouth must have opened, and my eyes got big. All I could say was, "oh my, oh my," page after page. I saw things I did not know existed. Mind you I was not living in a cave somewhere, but this was way outside of my purview. Surely, people never wanted anything in that area to be pierced. Just imagine the pain, that would be a deterrent enough, much less the exposure. I did not wait for the owner to finish with the client he had and return to us, I got out of there as quickly as I could. I did not want anything tattooed or pierced.

When we left Venice Beach I was still reeling from some of the things I saw on the beach and in the shops. We went to get dinner, not being familiar with the area I thought Jasmine could help decide on something amazing in Southern California. We couldn't agree on the local fare, but I suggested going to Olive Garden. After an experience like Venice Beach, I did not want anything I was unfamiliar with, no not this day.

On one of her early trips to Pittsburgh, she became hooked on Buffalo wings. She could eat them every day. On subsequent trips, she never forgot about the wings. It was like an addiction. Mom would make her a seven-up cake which she loved, and I think she may have taken the recipe back with her when she returned home. Not sure if she actually made the cake when she got home. At her home, her mom always made apple cobbler, and she was the best at it. Yum!

The next time she came was to her cousin Tai-Tanisha's wedding. They had become close, and my daughter wanted Jasmine to be in the wedding. She arrived at the last minute, and we raced around madly getting the last fittings for her bridesmaid's dress and accessories. The wedding was great, and the bridesmaids all cleaned up well.

After graduating from the University of California Santa Cruz, she did not have to rush back when she came to Pittsburgh. This time she stayed for quite some time. After completing her last class remotely while in Pittsburgh she decided to move to New York for more adventures. She and my mother bonded and became quite attached. Both mom and I both were sad that she was leaving us.

In New York, she met my sister-in-law Sylvia and her husband Carlos. They took her under their wings as far as acclimating her to the New York vibe. They shared their home with her in the Bronx.

Jasmine remembers the best times with us were talking, laughter, and food. Mom, Tai-Tanisha, and I never had an opportunity to spend time and get to know Jasmine until she was about twenty years old. That I consider a missed opportunity. Since then, we have caught up, enjoyed every moment with her, and look forward to many more joyful years. Mom loved and enjoyed getting to know her. Jack's other sons, Johnny and Lion, did not have a chance to spend time with us and get to know us well. We can put that on the bucket list for the future. I love you Jasmine, and much love to you Nini.

PART 8

Grandchildren

Jesus said, "Let the little children come to me, and do not hinder them, for the kingdom of heaven belongs to such as these."

Matthew 19:14 NIV

Not Your Friend...

Tai-Tanisha was in labor, and her child was coming soon. I was summoned to the hospital on a beautiful March day and arrived just in time. The doctor did not take long to announce, "it's a boy." The nurse carried him to a lighted table to get him cleaned up. I watched every move to make sure he was safe and to see what they were doing. The nurse asked, "Who are the parents?" He was so fair; she thought the child looked like he belonged to someone else. We assured her he was ours; she knew because she had seen my grandson, Rafael, born just seconds before.

As the years passed, Rafael and I, spent endless amounts of time together. We were besties. That is until Rafael did not get his way. He would threaten me by saying, "If you don't let me...., I am not going to be your friend anymore." Saying it over and over, thinking it would wear me out and I would give in. It never worked. With strong internal fortitude, I held my ground most of the time. Besides, he was so cute that I did not want to deny him anything.

My job sent me to Pittsburgh to see if I would accept a specific job as a promotion. I wouldn't say I liked the city, the environment, or the people in the office. I ultimately turned it down. A few weeks after returning to Denver, they begged me to go back and take another look at Pittsburgh. My grandson Rafael went with me. I revisited the office and spoke with some of the other managers. One manager, Bobbi, agreed to take me to lunch on Mt. Washington. We were the only two managers that seemed to have anything in common.

It was a spectacular day, and the weather was beautiful. We were seated at an outdoor table overlooking the confluence of the Allegheny, Monongahela, and Ohio Rivers. The food was good. Bobbi tried to talk to Rafael, but he would not speak to her. When we left the restaurant and headed home, Bobbi and I were stopped at a traffic light next to each other. Bobbi waved at Rafael from her car. He perked up, smiled, and waved back to her. He felt safe enough to communicate with her inside my car but didn't speak to her in person at lunch.

When Rafael was in the third grade, his dad, an MP in the army, was deployed during the school year. It was decided that he would stay with me until school was out in the summer. That way, he would not have to change schools in the middle of the school year. I spent my nights reading, doing bible study, and eating grapes in bed, sometimes late at night. He would sleep in my bed and eat grapes with me until his teacher told me, "please let that boy get some sleep and eat his grapes during the day so that he won't be tired in school."

My grandchildren would sometimes ask, "what are you about to do?" My answer was, "I am going to see my best friend," which was my bed. I consider myself a good sleeper. My sleep time happens opposite other family members, sleep times. I sleep on airplanes, on subways, and even while standing. I know how to "do" sleep. My daughter and I are the exact opposite, she is an early morning riser, and I get up late in the morning. Rafael is more like me. Maybe I broke him when he stayed with me to finish that school term.

Our youth group at the church scheduled a roller skating event at a nearby arena. All of the Sunday School children and their families were in attendance. Rafael was excited to go, but he had never learned to skate. He assured me he could do it, no problem. He is always self-confident. I like that about him.

Everyone split off and got their skates when we arrived at the arena. The music started, and the announcer told us what skaters were on the rink first, singles, couples, free skating, etc. After Rafael got his skates on and tied, he was ready to go. He went down as soon as he was on the rink, plop. He quickly got up and tried again, plop. Again and again, the same result. He was determined and refused to let this beat him. I started to feel bad for him, but I could not do anything. He would not quit. He is not a quitter, never has been, and never will be. I was not skating because skating was not my thing, and I did not want to find myself sitting on the floor every few feet, too.

My friend Leonora was an excellent skater. She was out there skating and having a good time. She recognized his problem and decided to help him get his flow and balance. They skated together. Rafael went down a few times but far less than before. After going around a few more times with Leonora, he seemed to have it together and was skating quite well. I looked around, it was as though he had been skating all his life. Amazing. He always had the abilities needed to master his interests in life.

Another beautiful day in Pittsburgh came when we were summoned to celebrate the marriage of Rafael and Raelyn. This was the first time meeting Raelyn, and she was so sweet. I remember meeting her grandmother through our church connections years before. Raelyn had asked me to quilt a blanket for the baby. I had the baby's name embroidered on it before Raelyn saw it. She loved it. I asked about the blanket one day. It has been put away for her to receive when she is older. Each grandchild and great-grandchild has been the recipient of a love quilt handmade by me.

Times Tables

I worked with Rafael's daughter, Ava'Marie, teaching her the times tables for her math class. It brought back the memory of me teaching them to her dad in the third grade. It was daunting. Every day Rafael and I went over them, and I taught him different strategies to help him remember. We practiced and practiced. We would have lots of progress and then some setbacks. What can I do to reinforce these times tables? I contacted some teachers and friends for tips on teaching them. I was about to pull out all my hair, trying to get him to learn these factors. I did my best. Giving him credit, I think he did his best, too. He still had a ways to go by the end of the semester.

He was to return to his parents for school in August. He was only with me to finish the school year. His parents were military, and you must go when Uncle Sam moves you.

Summer came, and I drove him to his new home in Louisiana. I know he missed his family, and I will be sad to see him go because we had a strong bond. I missed him tremendously.

School started in Louisiana, and I received a call from my daughter and was told that he had something to say to me. Rafael was so excited to tell me loudly, "grandma, I know my times tables, all of them." He finally got it after all our hard work. Why did he wait until he got there to get it? I did everything I could. I was so proud of him. Love you, Rafael & Raelyn.

P. S. The little hair I had left from pulling it out working on his times tables, I have pulled the rest out working with Ava'Marie doing the same. Deja vu.

This year one more grandchild, Sky, is in the third grade. I know it's times table time once again. Will I ever finish teaching the times tables? Who knows? Too bad I don't have any more hair to pull out. It should be smooth sailing without hair issues.

Fro

Thanksgiving morning, we woke up and lounged around like we always did, watching the Macy's Thanksgiving Day Parade and preparing for the big feast later in the day. When it was time for dinner, we helped ourselves to the feast. It had smelled good all day. But, just as soon as we took our first bites, Tai-Tanisha said, "it's time to go to the hospital," she was having labor pains. We took a few bites of our meal, grabbed our belongings and car keys, and took off for the hospital. We are about to have a Thanksgiving baby.

Later that day, we were introduced to our newest family member, Carlos. He was named after his grandfather, who was born on the same date; how lucky. By the time we got home, we were exhausted, and the food was cold. We decided to save all that good food for the next day, keeping the celebration of the new baby in our hearts for the night.

Squirrels

Most of the time, squirrels are pretty playful but won't let you get close. One summer in Kentucky, Carlos must have antagonized them.

They seemed to round up all the squirrels in the neighborhood and came back to attack Carlos. We still don't know the whole story. We saw the pack of squirrels chasing Carlos as he tried to get his glasses from the ground. Wouldn't you know it, one of the squirrels grabbed them and took off running in the opposite direction, with half of the pack following him and the other half chasing Carlos. We looked for those glasses until it was dark. He never got his glasses back and thank goodness the squirrels didn't catch and scratch or bite him. However, he won't turn his back on a squirrel to this day.

Zoo Keepers

During middle school, Carlos worked weekends at the Pittsburgh Zoo. He was a lover of animals and had the chance to feed, nurture and learn even more about different species. He was in his element. He earned the opportunity to travel to and attend the special Zoo Keepers Conference in Washington, D.C. He was excited to fly there and be with his group. However, his brother Rafael was graduating from high school simultaneously, and we all thought it essential for Carlos to be at the graduation, and attend the conference. We could make this happen.

His group flew from Pittsburgh to the conference in D.C. Carlos rode with us to Kentucky for the graduation. I called my friend Gwen who lives in D.C., I explained the conundrum. She welcomed the opportunity to help. Arrangements were made to get a flight out of Nashville the morning after the graduation. His group had arrived the night before, so he would not miss much.

The following day we rushed him to Nashville to catch the flight to D.C. Gwen picked him up at the airport and took him to the location of the Zoo Keepers Conference. When the conference was over, the group would fly back to Pittsburgh. We would be back to meet him in Pittsburgh on his return home. Everything worked out perfectly.

Homeschooled

One year in middle school, Carlos was homeschooled. He was excited about it and looked forward to doing school with me. He was up and ready, had breakfast, and was at the table prepared to learn before time. We did lessons, went to the library, took field trips, and lots more. On one field trip, I even learned something. It was the one where we went to the Lock and Dam. He was quite interested and later wrote an excellent report on what he learned. We rode down the river with Carlos assisting the Captain with some of the steering.

When the river's water is at different levels, the lock raises and lowers boats so they can continue their river journey. The boat sits in a stall, and water either fills up like a bathtub or is let out, so the boat can be lifted or dropped down. Leveling the boat with the water allows the boat to continue on a different river level. We had a first-class tour since we were the only ones at the Lock and Dam that day. An advantage of homeschooling versus a large group of students is that you have more private or one-on-one time on excursions.

Carlos passed homeschool with flying colors. That was probably his favorite school year. He bought a turtle and named him Naruto. For years he took good care of him. Later, after the military moved his family, he asked me to care for Naruto, and I did for a while. When I worked in an elementary school, I thought the turtle could be a blessing to the students in the science lab. Carlos was ok with that. I spoke to the science teacher; he thought it would be an excellent addition to their existing animals in the science room. The students loved Naruto. Naruto is still in that science room today. Carlos was happy the turtle would be loved and cared for in his absence. Having Carlos donate the turtle to the school gave him a sense of pride. Thanks for your heart, I love you, Carlos.

Ms. Vice President

$\mathcal{P}$ittsburgh turned out to be a blast, for real. Initially, I thought it was a smog-filled town with the sky always overcasts because of the steel mills in the area. It turned out that most of the steel mills were long gone. A different economy was established there. It was now more of an educational, medical, and research-driven industry.

My granddaughter was born there. The day her mom went to her check-up, the doctor sent her straight to the hospital, saying, "it's time." Mary, my daughter's mother-in-law, worked in labor and delivery at that hospital and was just about to get off work and head home. Of course, she stayed for the big event. After all, this was her grandchild being born. Again, it was time to welcome our newest family member, Michelle.

My daughter and her family were always coming to or leaving Pittsburgh for visits. I soon bought the best house money could buy. This gave us room for everybody when the family was staying there while my son-in-law was deployed. Sometimes they stayed for periods of a year or more. This happened more than once. The children attended several schools when living with me in the big house. On school days, I could watch Michelle and Carlos walk from the house down the hill until they were out of sight.

Michelle is the only girl with three brothers. I knew she needed to be involved and interested in some girl things. Some of my friends latched onto her and formed a Girls Club. She was about ten years old. Michelle looked forward to having girl time, learning, and discussing things that made her feel grown up and accepted. She learned exciting things that opened her eyes to many possibilities in the world. We discussed everything. Some women in the Girls Club were local, and others were in various states that I knew from work experience or were family.

Michelle took the lead on many occasions. We even elected her to be the VP of our group. The women on our conference calls were very diverse and shared various topics that a young girl might find interesting. There was much she could glean from our group; she loved it and ate it up. She looked forward, as we all did, to getting together often. She was made to feel like a much older girl and that her ideas were as important as any of our ideas. This experience has had an enormous influence on her life and could give her what she needs to pour into another little girl's life. You would make an excellent mentor.

Work Shadowing

After retiring from my career, I became a Mentoring Supervisor for at-risk children in the Christian community. Once when there was no school, she accompanied me to work at Family Guidance and spent the entire day there. She had a chance to explore the office and chitchat with some of the other workers. We had a pond in the back of our facility, and as a twelve-year-old, it drew her out to it. She probably wished she could take one of the ducklings home with her. We went to lunch with a couple of co-workers and enjoyed that. Michelle always had her ears open; I am sure she learned a lot that day.

The Proposal

After retiring a second time, I moved south. Michelle had graduated from high school and was attending college by this time. She informed me that her new, that is new to me, boyfriend was a soldier returning from a tour of duty in Korea and wanted to know if he could stay with me for a short bit. After discussing who he was, what he needed, and my house rules, I said it would be fine.

During Akeem's stay with me, we talked a lot because Michelle had school. We talked about him growing up and where he lived before becoming a soldier. He had lots of questions about not only Michelle but also our family. His stay was enjoyable. Michelle stayed there each night, also. Akeem did some cooking with Tai-Tanisha and prepared some of his favorites. He makes the best grilled jerk chicken on the planet.

Michelle and Akeem got up and out early, and I thought they were gone for the day. My apartment faced a pond with lots of ducks. Looking out the window across the pond, I could see them walking around it. Soon they returned. Michelle was so excited and called out, "grandma, grandma." I had no idea what was going on. She showed me that big ring on her finger and said, "Akeem proposed, and I said yes." She said he kneeled and everything.

This was magical, and I immediately said, "this needs to be captured on video." They had to go out and do it again so I could take pictures. Later in life, they will appreciate that memory being saved. It would have been lost if not captured then. She thought it was a little weird redoing the proposal. The pictures and videos came out perfectly. I know they will cherish them forever. I will never forget that moment, tears and all. The next step was to tell her mom, dad, siblings, and others. I sent them to do that alone. My part was done. The redo on the proposal indeed made for a better telling of the story both then and forever. I love you, Michelle and Akeem.

Brown Eyes

When Michael II (we call him Mikey) was about a year old, the family left Louisiana and Tai-Tanisha packed everything and closed the house; her husband was a deployed soldier in Korea. All of their belongings went into storage until he returned and had everything transferred to their new quarters on whatever military location he would be assigned.

She planned to drive to Pittsburgh with Mikey. Not wanting them to make that long trip alone, I decided to meet them halfway so I could help with the driving. Greyhound was the best option for me to connect with her. I determined that the approximate halfway point was Nashville, Tennessee. I found my best option by checking the drive time from Louisiana to Nashville and comparing it with Greyhound schedules. There would be a couple of transfers before arriving in Nashville. Taking this into account, I bought my ticket and communicated with her about the plan to meet in Nashville.

When I arrived in Nashville, Tai-Tanisha and Mikey were close, so I waited in the station until they picked me up. I don't think it was more than a half hour. Perfect timing. We met, ate, and found a hotel for the night. My mom was there when he was born. However, this was the first time I met my newest grandson. He had the most beautiful brown eyes and a calm spirit. He was a charmer. I gave him lots of hugs and kisses.

Inauguration

Mikey and I went to Washington, D.C., for the inauguration of President Barack Obama. We stayed with my friend Gwen and had a good time and even talked her into going to her first presidential inauguration. It was a history lesson for Mikey that he will never forget.

We took the train into the city from a nearby connection point close to Gwen's house. It was a near-perfect day. The sun was bright, and the sky was clear. It was a beautiful January day, with temperatures extremely mild for that time of year. When we arrived at our train stop, we walked and walked, trying to get as close as possible to get the best view. Neither Gwen nor I could get tickets for the seating area. We were happy to be able to attend an event like this, and I knew I would probably not get another opportunity like it again.

Mikey kept up. We found a good spot next to one of the jumbotron monitors overhead where we could see it all without anything or anyone blocking our view. Gwen and I tried to explain the significance of this historical moment to Mikey and the significance of President Obama being elected the first-ever African American President of the United States. He will be able to tell his kids and grandkids he was at the inauguration of the first Black President.

When the ceremony was over, Mikey suggested we get pizza on the way home. We had lots of time as we waited for the thick crowd to disperse. We knew that waiting on trains would take some time. So we sat and enjoyed our pizza to let the crowd thin out.

First Flight

The big day was finally here for us to travel to Italy. We got ready and left for the airport. His mother had prepared him a backpack to hold a change of clothes and small games to play while waiting for planes. We got our tickets and changed our money to Euros, Italian currency. Mikey and I were happy. However, our connecting flight to Detroit was delayed because of storms in Atlanta. When we missed our flight, that caused us to miss our plane to Rome. We got the next plane to Detroit an hour later. It was his first flight ever. He did not need a barf bag at all like he thought. It was a great experience. Mikey liked flying. Was he afraid? Not him.

After arriving in Detroit, we spent the night with family. Tomorrow we will get the next flight out to Italy. We saw no Italians or heard anyone speaking Italian on the big day, no not one. Ciao' Ciao'

We woke up early the following day and were ready to go to Italy once again. Arriving at the airport, we went through customs and security and had enough time for Mikey to get a strawberry shake from Starbucks. It was time to board. We flew first class. The pilot said the plane ride would be 8 hours and 15 minutes. Finally, we are in the air on our way to Rome.

Pinch me, we have landed at the Rome airport. First, we went through customs to check and stamp our passports and then to the baggage claim area. So many people were rushing to baggage claim, so you had to keep pace or risk getting run over. Trying to keep up with the flow of people was a challenge while making sure to keep holding Mikey's hand. His backpack was still on his back. The last thing I wanted to do was lose Mikey. I would never be able to go back home and confront my daughter and Michael.

My ponytail was clipped to the back of my hair. All of a sudden, it fell to the ground. So many people behind us were walking fast; they almost knocked me over as I bent to pick it up. I had to reach down and grab it quickly without missing a step, or we would have fallen on our faces. I quickly pinned it back onto my hair and kept walking. It was so fast that I am sure people around us never knew what had happened. Mikey wanted to laugh out loud but kept it to a solid smile. All is well today.

We waited at the carousel for more bags to come down the chute. We kept looking for our bags. Finally, there were no more bags. Realizing our bags were not there, we went to customer service and told them about it. They sent a note to Delta Airlines about the missing bags. We took the train into Rome without our bags and caught a cab to our hotel. He did well keeping up with his backpack.

We were at Hotel Medici at Via Flavia, 96, it was lovely. My friend Marsha was waiting for us in the patio area. She arrived the night before from Detroit. We rested, told Marsha about our luggage issue, and laughed. Sometimes all you can do is laugh.

Mikey found something interesting in the bathroom. He asked me about it as he tried to describe what he saw. It looks like a second toilet but had running water and did not flush. It was like a sink. I explained, "it is a bidet for washing and refreshing your butt."

Backpack

When Mikey was about three years old, my daughter Tai-Tanisha would drop him at Grandma Lillie's house so she could go to work. He was such a good kid, and very private, even as a youngster.

After Tai-Tanisha dropped Mikey off and left, he and my mom would have breakfast and sit to watch some children's programs. He would watch for a moment but then realize that his mom was gone. Mikey would get up, put on his backpack, and stand by the front door to my mom's apartment. He was not crying but silently waited by the door for his mom to return. My mom would try to get him to come back and watch his program using all sorts of tactics. She offered snacks, games, books, and other items to no avail.

She called his mom on the phone and let him talk to her. She told him to take his backpack off, put it near him, and sit and watch some of his favorite programs until she returned. He agreed. When he got tired, mom could see it in his eyes, but he was determined not to go to sleep at Grandma Lillie's house. He thought he might miss his mom picking him up and have to stay there. No matter how tired he got, he would not go to sleep and miss his ride. He was an obedient child and did just as his mom told him. This went on for many weeks.

One day he finally realized that he would get a call from his mom and that he was to sit, play, and watch television with Grandma Lillie until she came to pick him up. He no longer put his backpack on and stood by the door, waiting for his mom. She really was going to come back. She did every day. Love you, Mikey.

Decorations

Christmas was soon to arrive. I did not want to spend it in Pittsburgh without the whole family. My young cousin Kristia rode down with me to spend Christmas with family in Alabama. This was the first time Kristia would meet my grandchildren, and she was excited about traveling out of state.

We arrived safely. After hugging and kissing everyone, we settled in and prepared to do some sightseeing the next day. Kristia loved seeing new things and meeting new people. Those experiences changed her worldview tremendously. She soon moved to Alabama to live with my family and attend school there. She has been with the family ever since. In her heart, that was the best Christmas of all.

Kristia is the Christmas decorator extraordinaire. She has put her gifts to work, helping put up Christmas decorations at their house, at my house, and she has even traveled out of state to put her talents to work at Cousin Ida's house in Georgia. She and Mikey work on putting up their tree when it makes its way down from the attic at home. She won't stop until it is beautiful.

When she comes to my house, she immediately grabs everything from the garage and starts working on the tree. She even hangs glittery stars from my chandelier in the dining room. They look amazing. We work together to light up the hall's archway and put candles around the fireplace. Kristia doesn't stop there. She even puts lights on the small bushes in the yard, too. When it is done, it looks incredible. Cousin Ida always looks forward to getting inspiration and help from Kristia with her tree whenever we go to Atlanta.

Most of my grandchildren are adults and no longer travel with me to Atlanta for Thanksgiving. Kristia is still at home and is stuck with me asking her if she wants to go to Atlanta for Thanksgiving. She loves going with me. She has gone with me more than once and connected with Melissa, one of our cousins. They enjoyed spending time together, including doing one thing I hate "shopping." They shopped until they dropped. She always looks forward to us going again. Melissa visited us once, and we all went to the beach in Florida. That was fun.

Family Reunion

Family reunions were always something to look forward to every two years. It has been a while since I attended one. One reunion sticks out in my mind when Kristia and I drove to Mississippi to attend. It was a one-day trip, so we did not have to stay overnight en route.

On arrival, we put our things in our room and went straight to the reception. Meeting with family members I knew and getting acquainted with several new faces was exciting. They consider me the family historian. I always come prepared to connect people with their ancestors and answer any questions they may have. I bring a slide presentation to get everybody up to speed and a book with the generations that answer many questions. Kristia helped me just like she did in Michigan at the reunion a few years earlier. Kristia saw some relatives she knew from

Pennsylvania and hung out with them. We loved touring old cemeteries and learning about our family, especially from the newer attendees.

On the way home, we stopped as we arrived at the historic Edmond Pettus Bridge. We could not resist getting out and taking some pictures before we drove across it. I explained to Kristia the important history of that bridge. This is the bridge that years earlier Congressman John Lewis, Rev. Martin Luther King, Jr., and many others crossed during the Civil Rights Movement on what is known as "Bloody Sunday." It was an honor for me to walk in their footsteps, and because of their tenacity and fortitude, we have been given many of the freedoms our predecessors did not enjoy. Love you, Kristia.

Chica

Rafael, Tai-Tanisha's oldest, is the only one of her children who has kids. Ava'Marie is his oldest. We call her Chica. She and I have traveled extensively together. Ava loves traveling. She has gone to Denver, Atlanta, and many times to Alabama in a car, on the plane, and once on the Amtrak train.

Grandma Elizabeth

I visited Latoi (Ava'Marie's mom) in the hospital and met Ava'Marie when she was only one day old. Ava'Marie and I have been stuck together as if we were glued ever since. She affectionately calls me Grandma Elizabeth and has done so since she started talking. She calls my daughter, her grandma, Abuela. We call each other often. Now she is talking about going to her first school dance and what to expect. Oh boy, here we go again with firsts.

When she was only a few months old, I would sing "Jesus Loves You" to her every night until she drifted off to sleep. Ava'Marie quickly learned to walk and talk. Sometimes I would pick her up from daycare, and when she saw me, she would run and give me a big hug. Latoi was happy to see how we sang, played, and spent time together.

Vitamin C

One year I drove to Alabama for the Christmas holiday, and only Ava'Marie was with me. Rafael and Latoi had to work and couldn't get off. On the way, she slept a lot since it was such a long drive, about fourteen hours. Ava'Marie was a good baby and never cried or got upset. At one juncture, she woke up. I thought she was still sleeping until I heard her say from the backseat, "All Gone." Immediately I pulled over. I didn't have time to wait for the next exit. What was all gone? There was nothing back there with her. Once I got out and opened the back door, I saw she had gotten my chewable Vitamin C tablets from my purse near the center console, and the container was empty. I called my daughter and told her. We prayed that she would be fine. Next, I called the poison control center to see if there was any danger in her eating all of the chewable Vitamin C tablets. Thank goodness there were only a few in the bottle. I explained her age and how many she had. They assured me she would be fine.

Ava'Marie and Molly, our family dog who is gone now, were best friends. When she heard that Molly had passed, she was shaken. They played together almost as much as siblings and sometimes better than siblings. Molly was with us even before Ava'Marie was born. She had known Molly her entire life.

Virtual Classroom

Latoi asked me if Ava'Marie could come and spend time with me to do virtual school during the pandemic. I said, "absolutely." She was here three days later. We did schoolwork, talked, and prayed together each night. We went out for smoothies at lunchtime as often as possible. She loves them. It was a blessing for Latoi to ask me to do something that I was grateful for the opportunity to do. Latoi trusts Abuela and me with her daughter, and we are thankful for that. I love you, Latoi. Ava'Marie is the spitting image of her Abuela, Tai-Tanisha, not only in looks but in personality. She is Abuela's mini-me.

I remember a time just recently when Ava'Marie was experiencing some students fighting on the school bus and was not comfortable. She called me from her cell phone on FaceTime, and I talked to her until she reached her stop. Thank goodness for one good purpose for those cell phones. I am glad I was available since both mom and dad were at work. She knows she can call me at any time, and she does. Love you, Ava'Marie.

Huggable

Raelyn, Rafael's wife, was excited and hoped that the baby would come soon. She was experiencing labor pains and would soon be going to the hospital. I knew the baby was ready to come and wanted to get to Pittsburgh in time. My bags were packed, and after bible study, all that was needed was to get to sleep. I would leave Alabama in the morning. My friend Silby would help me drive and keep me company on the two-day journey. I learned long ago to break the trip in half, get a hotel for the night, and be refreshed. It has become too much for a one-day trip.

Pittsburgh at last. The baby was already here, so we went directly to the hospital. Raelyn was exhausted, and Rafael was asleep on the couch like he had done the hard work of delivering the baby. No baby was in sight. The nurses brought the baby in within a few minutes. Raelyn introduced me to Ka'Rina. She was adorable. Very peaceful and just huggable. Silby and I stayed a while and then let the mother, father, and baby get some rest. We went to get something to eat, dropped Silby at her hotel, and I went to their house to stay with Gaven and Sky, Ka'Rina's older siblings.

For the next three months, Ka'Rina and I bonded and spent every day together, especially after Raelyn returned to work. The hardest part of the trip was going up and down the steps with her, and my aching knee. I was determined not to drop her. My goal was to do those stairs only once a day. We came down in the morning to get Gaven and Sky to their school bus and did not go back upstairs until bedtime.

When it snowed, the baby got a good look at the snow, and her eyes were big, bright, and full of interest. I remember the first time Ka'Rina saw snowflakes, and a few fell on her nose before we reached the car and fastened her in her car seat. She was only a few months old, but there was an obvious wonderment on her face. These were precious months with Gaven, Sky, and Ka'Rina. I think those months solidified Ka'Rina's and my relationship. Ka'Rina and I spent our days together reading, singing, and napping. Even now, when she hears my voice on the speakerphone with her mom or dad, she says, "Hi, Grandma Letha." She knows the voice from when she was only a few months old. I sang Jesus Loves You to her every day, morning and night, just as I did for Ava'Marie when she was the same age. If they didn't know anything else at that age, they knew that song and the sound of my voice. I love you, Ka'Rina.

Gaven and Sky

Rafael and Raelyn married several years ago, and I was fortunate to attend the celebration with all the family. That is where I first met Raelyn and her two older children, Gaven and Sky. I have enjoyed getting to know them. Since then, God has blessed them with another child, Ka'Rina.

I remember when I went to Pittsburgh for Ka'Rina's birth. That was when I had a chance to spend lots of time getting to know Sky and Gaven. Sky thought it was great to share her room with me. When mom and the baby came home from the hospital, I did all I could to assist with the two older children and do some household duties. Each morning, I got the children up, drove them to the school bus stop, and waited for the bus to arrive. In the afternoon, I did just the reverse. Sky is looking forward to visiting me in Alabama one day.

After their snack, we immediately got busy doing homework. Sky is teaching herself to speak Spanish. She has learned several phrases and words. I want her to take an actual class one day. It will be offered in middle school in a couple of years. Until then, I will encourage and help when I can.

Gaven was usually caught up with most of his homework before he got home from school. He did not have much of it left to do. Once their homework was completed, signed, and returned to their backpacks, they went outside to play. Most children are happy not going outside to play anymore. Video games and other electronic devices are all the rave. Don't get it twisted. They also liked video games, especially Gaven. After dinner, if there was still a little time before bed, Gaven grabbed his controller and got a few games in.

Sky was always willing to get things for me when I wanted something from upstairs and needed an extra pair of legs. She was a dutiful helper. She even helped with the baby and liked to hold and feed her. My friend Iris and I would take the children to church on Sundays. Sky was always excited to go and prepared herself by picking out her favorite dress each week. When I picked them up after church was over, she couldn't wait to tell all about what she learned in her class, and Gaven too. There was always an incentive to stop for hamburgers or other snacks after church. They both liked that.

I took them to the art store to buy, design, and paint their own artwork for their parents as Christmas presents. A week later we went back to pick them up after they had been baked in a kiln. Everything was beautiful. When their parents opened Their parents loved the gifts when they opened the on Christmas morning.

The children each have a cell phone, and sometimes I will call them individually and chat for a few minutes. Sky talks and tells me about school and other activities she does. Gaven is a man of few words. It takes work to engage him in a lengthy conversation. He answers your question and is ready to move on. Ka'Rina is three now and is also beginning to like talking on the phone. She explains things well and is pretty easy to understand. Soon I won't be able to keep her quiet.

I love my great-grandchildren and look forward to many more memories and conversations with them.

I know for sure I will hear from them if there is homework that they are struggling with, they call me, and I am eager to help. Every day I pray for God's blessings over all the children for learning, obedience, growth, and safety. I love each of them in their own unique way. Love you Gaven and Sky.

Every day I pray for God's blessings over all the children for learning, obedience, growth, and safety.

PART 9

Work/Friends

My people will live in peaceful dwelling places, in secure homes, in undisturbed places of rest.

Isaiah 32:18 NIV

Afternoon Dining

Koinonia happens in different places. Each of our group had a favorite spot to go to. We would rotate. An establishment would not want us there too often, thinking, "here's that group that takes up a table for hours at a time." These were lovely upscale places. They allowed us to reward our palate with differing and exceptional dining cuisines. You could smell the goodness and hear and feel the friendliness of other patrons as you walked in. The courteousness of the staff was as important as the food itself. It had to be clean, and cloth tablecloths were a must. Seats by the window and a view were important. But best of all, you can not beat sitting outside, overlooking the Three Rivers, at a restaurant on Mt. Washington in Pittsburgh. The aura of outdoor eating and fellowship makes you lose track of time when the weather is superb. If I close my eyes and think of one of those times, it just makes me shiver and smile.

Sometimes we would be at one place for lunch and were still there when the dinner crowd began arriving. We saw couples and families with children and ladies on a girl's day out. We only saw a few guys at these restaurants with their families. Men don't think much about going out to eat in the afternoon with the boys or having cloth tablecloths.

Once, we saw a table of Red Hat Ladies dining together. The Red Hat Society is a worldwide organization where members gather to celebrate every stage of life. They find ways to celebrate each other by sharing food, traveling, going to plays, and other activities. We took a moment to talk to them. They liked that we recognized and knew their mission.

A couple of ladies formed a second Koinonia. We typically went to the same restaurant each time we went out. Their palate was not as particular as the other group of ladies. As long as they got chicken, all was well in the world. However, the time spent dining and talking was equally as long and enjoyable.

Moving around town in search of unique places was fascinating. Some places were recommended by word of mouth. Others were researched online or noticed when driving by, coupled with a sixth sense. We were always satisfied. Traveling across the country for work allowed me to compare different styles and tastes. Each state had specialties developed by the culture of its society. We could have signed on as some of the next great "food critics." Establishments should have thanked us for spreading the word about the food and ambiance of their restaurant. It was never cheap, but worth it.

Baby, It's Cold Outside

Songs are a great memory trigger. Whenever my friend Margaret hears, "Baby, It's Cold Outside," I can expect to receive a call. When she called, we always talked and laughed about the song and ended up talking about going to get chicken. There is a funny story behind hearing this song, a car ride, and extreme weather. Some things are funnier when left to your imagination.

Margaret is raising her granddaughter Dalis. Dalis and Ava'Marie have been best friends since they were babies. They both traveled to visit me since I moved south. Ava'Marie and Dalis were so glad to see each other again and had the best time running, talking, playing, and swimming. I hope they will come again soon.

I have been trying to coach Margaret into writing a book. She has the whole book already in her mind. She even has the title picked out. Once she sits down and starts writing, it will flow like a river.

Iris

Getting together is only sometimes possible in person. My friend Iris is still thinking about coming south for a visit. When I visited Pittsburgh, she and I took my great-grandchildren to her church each week and then out to get a snack before returning home. They loved it. When I lived in Pittsburgh, we liked to go to Chucky Cheese for lunch, and we spent much time there in conversation. By the way, Iris and I were the only ones there without any children. We just loved their hot wings.

We talk on the phone weekly, laughing and sharing things about our grandkids and children. Iris is a fantastic painter using watercolors to produce exceptional paintings. Her daughter and I believe her works should be sold, but she is storing them to share on special occasions. They will be gifts of love.

Big Sky Country

Flying to Montana to a customer site for a system cutover, I rode an eighteen-seat plane with nine seats on one side of the aisle and nine on the other. This has to be the smallest plane in the commercial line. The plane jerked fast and sharp as we approached the destination, rising upward and turning sharply. Everything on my tray table flew up and then crashed. Grabbing the arms of the seat, I began to pray, knowing we had just had a near-miss plane crash. Thank goodness the pilot was alert and made the correction before a tragedy occurred. God was indeed with him.

Speaking of food on the tray table, yes, there was food even in the coach section on domestic flights. With nine seats on each side of the aisle, you could still consider having a coach section. In the past, all mealtime flights (breakfast, lunch, and dinner) served a full-course meal including bread, rolls, meat, vegetable, starch, dessert, and beverage. You even had a choice of which meal you preferred, meat, chicken, fish, or vegetarian. Get this; it came with the ticket at no additional charge. This would never happen today. Getting a beverage to each passenger is almost impossible before you have to gulp it down because we are about to land. Plus, you pay a hefty fee if it's more than a soda or juice. There may be meals in first class on domestic flights. I wouldn't know since I fly coach.

After we landed, I rented a car and drove about eighty-five miles the remainder of the way. There was sagebrush blowing along the desolate road, animals in the fields, and various crops that I could not identify. My destination was only forty minutes from the Canadian border.

There were no major hotel chains in this small town. My accommodations included a room upstairs from the bar that also included a restaurant. While settling for the night above the bar, cowboy music played, and I assumed there was dancing and drinking downstairs. Music was played at a decent level and ended by ten o'clock. Most of the town were farmers and would want to turn in early. Each morning I would get ready, go down to the bar, and order breakfast.

It could be eaten in or taken out. Takeout was not a good idea because I would have to eat at my client's office. Once I arrived at the customer site, I would be ready to do training and manage the job.

That whole week I saw no one that was a part of my culture. However, I received a warm welcome, and everyone was pleasant. Over the weekend, I drove around the countryside. Later, in town, I did a little shopping at the ma and pop shops. There was no sales tax in Montana at that time. Whatever the price tag said was precisely what you paid. This was the first time I had shopped in a tax-free environment. There were no malls or chain stores of any kind. The only eating establishment was the bar under the room I rented.

After ten days, the job was completed. I spent the time managing the system upgrade and incorporating the company's new requirements. The customer was satisfied, and the system technicians and I prepared to leave. I was sorry I never got to go to the Canadian border while I was so close. I took the road back through farmland with crops, animals, and farmhouses. Yes, and there was still sagebrush in the road. Arriving at the airport, I turned in the car and prepared to board the small plane for home. Hopefully, there will be no near-miss collisions on the way back.

Conference Connection

Mom always wanted to accompany me when I traveled for work. I brought her with me when I did not have to fly to the destination. She would call to confirm the arrangements for my trip so she could let the ladies in her building know her travel schedule. She would say, "I will be out of town on business." Mom was a professional to them. They anxiously looked forward to hearing about her exploits. I am sure she added a little something-something to the story to make it good and juicy.

This trip was to Baltimore and D.C. Mom knew she would be in the hotel all day while I was working or in meetings, and that was OK with her. She had everything she wanted. When my workday was over, I would pick her up at the hotel and take her for a wonderful dinner and some sightseeing. Knowing the drill, she prepared herself with snacks and other things to keep her for the day.

I first met Gwen at a team meeting where she recognized her church's emblem on my tote bag. We discovered we had our church denomination in common. My friend Leonora and I had gone to a church conference in D.C., where I had purchased the tote bag. I didn't meet Gwen until we were on the same work team—small world.

One time, I took Rafael to work with me in Baltimore; he knew I would be in meetings. He took his skateboard and other things to keep busy. My team could look out the conference room window and watch him skate. He was delighted. Both mom and Rafael knew that when they went to work with me, we would go out later and have whatever they wanted for dinner and treats.

Libya

One of the many things I valued in fellowship was spending time with my mentee, Libya. I was matched with her when she was eleven years old. We explored dining out, cooking in, theatre, local activities, and traveling together. I picked her up after work and asked her where we wanted to eat. She would name one of the traditional fast food joints, and I usually suggested something new and different for her to try. She would sometimes turn her nose up at places like the Olive Garden and Red Lobster. Once we got there, she would study the menu for a long time trying to find something that she could recognize. Some weeks we would go to the grocery store and buy items for us to cook at home, she liked that. Each week we tried new things for her palate. Soon, she became quite the connoisseur and a good cook. We continued to eat out, and she began to order things she never had and ultimately enjoyed them.

The first time she went outside of the city limits where she was born was to my family's house in Kentucky. She met my grandchildren who were about her same age and was able to build a long-standing friendship with them as well. I showed her how to read a map and the road signs. I gave her a choice of doing the driving and I would give the directions, or she could read the map, and I would drive. She picked reading the map and reminded me she was only eleven and did not drive. Her assignment on the nine to ten hour trip was to give me directions. I even told her if she gave me the wrong information we would never get to my daughter's house and possibly end up in the wrong state. She was laser focused after that statement. We made it without a problem. Of course, I knew the way, and we would not have gotten lost.

During our time together we went to plays, skating, bowling, and holiday events. Whenever there was school parent-teacher conference and recitals at school, I would make it my business not to miss any of them. We enjoyed a lot of the same things, and our tastes melded incredibly well.

We still call each other and update our lives often. She is married now and has children of her own. Libya and Sam have been married close to or a little more than ten years. I just learned that her daughter was a cabin mate with my great-granddaughter Ava'Marie last summer at camp. Who would have thought, all this from a mentoring match?

She has several degrees and is working towards her doctorate. Thank God he put us together and I don't know if our relationship moved her to the success she has accomplished, but maybe it did just a little. Libya has always been a beautiful girl with an exceptional personality. I enjoyed our time together, and look forward to many more years of friendship. I love you Libya, I am so proud of you.

Cougar Convention

Marsha and I have known each other since first grade. We know each other well and each other's family, too. We graduated together, and we went to prom together with our dates. We know each other's antics, and there is always something up. We know each other so well that her grandchildren call me the "good grandma," my grandchildren think the same of her. We talk every week. There is always something to discuss when you have known someone for over sixty-five years. God sometimes puts people in your life for a reason, a season, or a lifetime. She is definitely a lifetime friend.

Marsha and several ladies from her church in Detroit had planned for months to attend the Sight-Sound Theater in Lancaster to see one of the current shows. This theater performed many superb biblical-themed stage productions. People from around the country attended these shows. In the past, when I had gone, I saw large buses from almost every state on the east coast and in the midwest. These productions were well-known in the Christian community for their exceptional work.

Marsha and I talked about how they had to come past my city, and I immediately suggested they stop for lunch with me instead of eating turnpike food. Near the third exit on the Pennsylvania Turnpike was a nice restaurant with a unique ambiance, friendly staff, and reasonably priced food. After discussing it with the ladies and the bus company, they agreed this would be great. Directions were given to them, and we all awaited the day. Coordinating their leaving time and estimating how long before they would arrive in my city was done by both of us.

Arriving early at the restaurant, I told the hostess about the event and the number of people attending. They immediately began setting the side room up with enough seating for about twenty people. The hostess was aware of their estimated arrival time. They sat me in the room that was set up for the group. I told them the group's name was the "Cougar Convention, and they said, "great." I had time for an iced tea or two before I heard several people talking and laughing and assumed it was my group. They all turned the corner into the room.

Marsha looked like she was going to strangle me as she laughed. Everybody was laughing and pointing at me. They said, " boy are you going to get it!" I asked, with a furrowed brow, "what is the problem.?" They all chimed in simultaneously, "COUGAR, how dare you!" Marsha introduced everyone. Soon we ordered our meal. They couldn't stop talking about the joke, but eventually, they had to finish eating and get back on the turnpike for the balance of their journey.

I always find my way to her church when I am in Detroit. As I slip in quietly, her pastor, no matter what, calls me out by name from the pulpit with a greeting. I am definitely one of his flock. Thanks, Pastor Morales.

Even today and probably forever, the ladies at her church will ask her, "how is the Cougar Convention lady?" They don't even know my name, so sad. Blessings to you, Marsha, my forever friend.

Escalators

Immediately after my husband passed, I needed some documents from our safe deposit box at the mall. Normally I used the neighborhood branch, so I was not familiar with this location. Emily, Leon, and I were wandering around searching for my bank at the mall. Leon was a close friend of my husband. We all hung out, more than we probably want to remember. We regularly did wild and crazy things, and laugh our heads off. We split up, looking for the bank. Leon and I kept trying to find Emily once we found the bank. Of course, I would have called her and given our location if cell phones had been invented. This was nineteen seventy-four. We had never heard of cell phones then.

Soon I spotted her, and she saw me at the same time. Emily was upstairs on the top level, and we were downstairs on the lower level. She immediately started to join us by jumping on the escalator. Unfortunately, she jumped on the escalator that was coming up as she was trying to go down, walking faster and faster to overcome the speed so she could change the gravity of the situation. We all laughed and laughed. This became a revisited story for a long time. Leon has not ever let her live that down. She had recently received her graduate degree (Ph.D.). They didn't teach her that to get to the lower level by escalator, you must take the down escalator. That should have been a prerequisite for the degree. So funny. I am envisioning the sight now as I am typing this story. Ha, Ha.

Westward Move

My sister-friend, Emily, was always there and immediately became Aunt Emily to my daughter. Emily received a great job opportunity and was preparing to move to North Carolina. We went almost everywhere together, and even though I was happy with her accomplishments, it made me sad. My running buddy will be gone. Shortly after, my request to transfer to Michigan was approved, and preparations to pack and move to Detroit were made and achieved. Both of us had now left New York.

She thoroughly enjoyed her new assignment, the people, and the community. This was laid back compared to New York, with less hustle and bustle getting around. There were no frustrations in driving because the drivers seemed more courteous and respectful.

A Ph.D. can open up many doors; in Emily's case it did, resulting in her next position in Denver. I was living in Detroit at that time. She called and shared her excitement about the new offer in Denver and asked if I would be willing to help her drive across the country to take that new job. The moving company would take care of all the belongings; the only thing left was driving the car to Denver.

The date was coordinated, and the time arrived for Tai-Tanisha and me to fly from Detroit to North Carolina. We helped Emily finalize that chapter in her life before beginning our drive to Denver. I knew nothing about Denver except what I had seen in a few western movies. One movie I liked a lot was the *Unsinkable Molly Brown*. Molly survived the horrific sinking of the ship Titanic. Molly Brown lived in Denver, and her home was a tourist attraction that we visited while we were there.

On each leg of the trip, we found a memory to capture on film, actual film, not cell phone pictures. Before we could see them, they had to be dropped off for development. We took pictures of historic places: the sign that says "welcome to _____," in each state we entered, the Mississippi River sign, and the Gateway Arch in St. Louis. The Mississippi river was east of the Arch. This represents the dividing line between the Eastern half of the United States and the Western half. Every time we entered a new state, we said, "yay, we are in_____." Most of those states I had never been in before. Pictures were taken of each sign and monument.

While in Denver, we did lots of sightseeing. The city was new to all of us; it was a beautiful place. The temperature was in the mid-nineties every day, with almost no humidity. One afternoon we went into the Rocky Mountains and drove up Berthoud Pass. As we climbed, we unconsciously began to turn the air-conditioning down, little by little. The next thing you know, we had turned it completely off. It was cold. Going to the top of Berthoud Pass was one of the more popular tourist activities. It is beautiful and is on the Continental Divide. The elevation at the top is 11,307 above sea level. The divide means that water from one side of this point drains to one ocean, and water on the other side drains to another. On one side of the pass, the water drains to the Pacific Ocean and on the other side to the Atlantic Ocean. We all got out at the top and had our picture taken next to the sign that marks the point.

There was snow on the ground, and Tai-Tanisha (about seven years old) could not resist making a few snowballs. We tossed one or two at each other until we were so cold we couldn't wait to get back in the car and put the heat on. Remember we started the day in sleeveless clothes since it was in the mid-nineties when we left home. As we descended the mountain after such a memorable day, we realized it was getting warm in the car. Turning off the heat and eventually putting the air back on was necessary.

The remaining days in Denver sold me on moving there, too. We visited the United States Mint, where coins are made, the Molly Brown House, Ski Chalets, the Mile High Marker on the steps of the state capital, and many other places. The more I saw, the more I was sold on moving to Denver.

When I returned to Detroit, I couldn't stop thinking about my Denver trip. A year later, I put in a request to transfer to Denver. Amazingly it was approved in record time. I would have never known the beauty of Denver and its attraction had I not had this incredible opportunity to visit there with Emily. They wanted to fill other open positions in Denver that I shared with another person in my office, who also transferred there. Some of the family helped us pack and prepare to move.

The day finally came; the moving van was here. Our belongings were packed and gone by nightfall. All that was left was to say our goodbyes and hit the road. My husband is going sight unseen. The drive took us past some familiar landmarks we passed on our first trip to Denver with Emily. We saw different historical sights en route. My husband had lots of questions, and I had plenty of answers. We took our time and enjoyed the journey. We stopped for the night and chose cities with well-known dining places. Having heard about some of the Bar-B-Q places in St. Louis, we chose one for dinner.

On day three, we arrived in Denver and took a deep breath at the sight of the Rocky Mountains and the exciting vibe of the city. Speaking of breath, we quickly learned how winded you could get there because of the altitude, for the first few days. Since I was transferring my job, we made sure to find my work location and how to get there as we toured. My husband would be looking for a new job.

Tai-Tanisha and I would discover the city by selecting a few different bus lines and riding them from end to end to see all we could take in since I was not driving. We did this every weekend. The townhouse we lived in was near a mall where several bus lines terminated, making it easy for us to choose different lines to try each week. We quickly learned the city layout.

We loved Denver so much and decided this would be an extended stay. The decision was made to purchase a home. This was a huge decision, and we did not want to take it lightly. Neither my husband nor I had ever owned a home before. I never even had the thought. My mom and her sisters were the first in the family to be homeowners, but being young, the thought had never crossed my mind. Once the decision was made, we began saving and putting aside all we could for our new purchase. There were sacrifices made, but we hung tough.

Taking the bus to work each day, I observed some new condominiums and townhomes going up and decided to check them out one evening. We all went to look at the models and toured the units and talked about the money needed to purchase one. They were amazing. I never envisioned being able to afford one of these. How awesome that we could customize the build and make it just like we wanted. No one had ever lived in this house, and it would be designed just for us. Could we do it? I prayed hard. The decision was made to fill out the paperwork and wait for approval. It did not take long before approval was given.

On Sundays after church, Tai-Tanisha and I would drive by the construction site and see the progress of the work. Each week I was amazed at how much had been accomplished since the previous week.

I noticed there should have been a window on the side wall, and it was not there. I called our contact person, and they immediately fixed it.

Completion was getting closer and closer. It was time to discuss the furnishings and what color paint, countertops, carpet, and other items we wanted to be installed. The most interesting question was whether we wanted air-conditioning and a microwave above the stove. I called my husband, and he said we wanted air-conditioning, but he did not think we needed the microwave. I did not know anyone who had a microwave. The lack of humidity in Denver made air-conditioning optional. I called the lady and advised her that we wanted air-conditioning and the microwave. Since he wanted and got air-conditioning, I decided I wanted the microwave.

The local appliance store offered classes on how to use a microwave, and I signed up for the class. I learned to do things that we don't even use in today's world. For example, they taught us to make a cake, brown meat, and other things in the microwave. That is not what I use my microwave for today.

It was only a short time before our home was completed, and we moved in. What a wonderful day, I could not stop pinching myself. A new home no one had ever lived in before. I had a fireplace, laundry room, garage, balcony, unique fixtures, and a microwave. Each bedroom had a bathroom, and there was a powder room on the first floor. Growing up, I remember there was one bathroom for the entire house and in the basement was just a toilet. Those were the old days, no one will have to wait now. I breathed in deeply to get the new house smell every day. What a blessing. Thank you, Lord.

One morning I was vacuuming upstairs, and suddenly, I heard a tink, tink sound coming from down in the kitchen and realized it was my husband pushing buttons on MY microwave. I ran down and asked what he was trying to do. He had not taken the classes and had not asked me any questions about how to use the microwave. I handled what he needed, gave him a brief review of the microwave, and told him that he was not to use it until I thought he was trained well enough to do so and not blow up the house. He agreed.

Since then, every house I have lived in has had air-conditioning and a microwave. Now, I could not live without either of them. This house was so majestic in my mind that I could not have asked for anything more. Since then, I have owned other homes, but the first one was special. The one in Pittsburgh was not new; it was in perfect condition, with everything that was in the first house and more. The one I own now was built for me. Again I visited throughout the construction process and watched with amazement the progress made each week. This house is just as impressive in a different way. When I moved in, I walked through and breathed deeply to enjoy the newness. No one had ever lived here either. Another blessing. What have I done to deserve love like this? Thank you, God.

$75 a Week

New York, the city so nice they had to name it twice, New York, New York. Bright lights and lots of excitement were calling my name. Becoming a Laboratory Technician and working in a large hospital was not enough for me. I liked my work and planned to continue that in New York. But, when I got there, a few additional credits were needed to get a New York technician license. Living arrangements and more classes cost money that I did not have. To survive, I had to get other work for the time being. I could not wait on additional college credits. The plan was to get a job and save for those classes down the road, so I did.

I started working immediately as a line assignment clerk for New York Telephone Company on E. 42nd Street. This job started me on a career path to retire thirty-six years later from the communications industry and not from a hospital. My responsibility was to find available telephone numbers that could be assigned to orders for new service. Some of my co-workers took me under their wing. Many became lifelong friends. My partner (who became my sister-in-law) sat next to me and taught me everything I needed to know for the job. We covered for each other during break time and lunch. Covering her phone when Sylvia was at lunch or break allowed me to get to know her brother Carlos when he called. We talked like we were old friends until she returned to her desk. One day he came to see her, and we finally met. Soon we were going to lunch together, and after some time, we began dating and ultimately married.

I made more money as a new hire than I did doing laboratory work in a hospital. Being comfortable with my salary and only working weekdays, unlike the hospital, where I worked every weekend, was a blessing. The salary was terrific. That was my initial belief.

My weekly salary was seventy-five dollars a week. That was far more than most people I knew made. When I received a raise making one hundred dollars a week, I thought I was rich. I called home and was excited to share my success with my mom. She was pleased. I later heard the news reporter discuss the poverty rate and income. Paying close attention to his report to see where my hundred-dollar-a-week salary fit, I was appalled to hear that I was in poverty when I thought I was rich. That was an eye-opener. Even though my hundred-dollar-a-week salary went a long way, it was still low on the totem pole in the big scheme of things.

After more than a decade with New York Telephone Company, and having worked in many different locations in Manhattan, I transferred to Michigan Bell Telephone Company. I moved to a different position where I no longer assigned single numbers on orders, but large orders for business customers. Several years later, I moved to Colorado and transferred to Mountain Bell. Each time I moved, I received promotions and pay increases.

The communications industry was taking on a new dimension where competitive companies could move into the market. I worked with the competitors to fill their orders for phone numbers. Later, divestiture occurred when the government made it the law for competition to infiltrate the industry. At this time, the company split, and employees were asked to select Mountain Bell or AT&T. I chose AT&T and moved to a different position and location. In September of 1996, another split occurred where AT&T split again, forming Lucent Technologies. I choose Lucent Technologies.

Managing fifteen male technicians would be one of my first and favorite positions. This was my first role as a managing supervisor, and they accepted me immediately, and we developed a mutually respectful working relationship. I held many corporate positions and did a lot of ladder climbing in many locations during my career. All of these positions were offered one after another with significant pay increases each time.

After graduating from the University of Denver, I was offered a position as a Customer Educator and Systems Consultant. My clients were large business customers who wanted to embark on new technologies. I met with managers to understand the business, uncovered how they communicated now, and suggested new ways their new system could improve their operations. All programming, needs assessment, restricting access where required, and training was on my plate. My service area included Idaho, Montana, Wyoming, and Colorado.

Lucent Technologies transitioned to Avaya, and that was the last company split in my career. It was all the same as far as seniority and time worked were concerned. God blessed me with a career I could not have imagined, never knowing these positions existed. If asked as a young child, "What do you want to be when you grow up?" This career could not have formed in my mind.

Rental Car Woes

Traveling on my job was extensive. Once I was doing some training in Dallas and was called by a co-worker to help in New York. My work in Dallas could be wrapped up the next day, and I said I would join them in New York. My flight was booked, and I turned in my rental car, boarded the plane, and went to sleep, as usual, until we arrived in New York. Getting my luggage was no problem, and the van took me to the rental car lot.

The rental car company would not give me a car because they said I already had one. I asked, "do you think I put the other one on the plane? I turned it in at the Dallas airport before boarding." Dallas had a backlog of returned cars, and I had been instructed to drop the car in a particular lane and leave the key inside with the motor off. It just so happened that my plane reached New York before they could process the cars in the drop-off section in Dallas. They did give me a car after checking in with their Dallas office. At that time in my career, it was as if I was traveling at the speed of light. I couldn't get a car in one city because the dropped-off car had not been processed in the previous one.

At a different time, also in New York, we rented a car and chose to venture off to Brooklyn to get some of the best cheesecake in the world from Junior's. They are pretty well known for their sweet fare. We thought it would be quick, but quite a few people were ordering. Also, more than one of us read the parking sign, and we must have all failed reading in elementary school. The sign did not say what we thought. We realized we had misread it when we returned to get in, and the car was gone. It had been towed. In New York, you can imagine that retrieving a car from the towing company was expensive, and there was much delay with deliberately slow personnel. New Yorkers talked fast, but that's the only thing they did fast.

With much a-do and much a-Doe (money), we got the car and returned to Junior's to get everybody else. Thank goodness we had our Junior's cheesecake. Yay, Junior's! I couldn't wait to turn in that rental car.

Smart Car

Have you had a new car lately? I recently acquired one, and boy, are things very different from earlier cars that I owned. People talk about their smartphones; I call it my smart car. This car could probably even write this book. I can speak, and it will do things with the key, never leaving the inside of my purse. I can start it from my dining room table. Letting down the windows to cool it off from inside the house and turning the air conditioning on before you get in makes life great in the summer months. The ability to warm or cool the car before you get in; that's what I call comfort. It can do so much more, even stop itself before you hit someone or something.

Sending a text message is easy when you speak what you want the text to read. Speak your directions, and the car goes into navigation mode immediately. No key is needed in my hand to open or lock the car. After having this car for a couple of months, I finally remember to turn it off when I get out.

Hybrids enter silent battery mode when stopped at lights, and in preparation to exit the car. After I start from a light, it needs to get back up to forty miles per hour before you hear the motor come back on, as it switches back to gas.

If the key in the bottom of my purse gets too far from the car as I leave it, the car will lock itself. Now, that's a smart car, smarter than some people I know. Attempting to discover all of the beautiful things my new car is capable of overwhelmed me. I soon closed the huge manual and tucked it away in the glove compartment, never to come out again. There are so many options, and I am okay if I can do some new things. I will never need or use all of the features. One of my favorite new features is seeing the speed limit sign on my dashboard. When the speed changes, I no longer have to notice the posted road sign it changes on my dashboard. How innovative. I can no longer use the excuse of not knowing the speed limit. That excuse goes right out the window.

PART 10

School

If any of you lacks wisdom, you should ask God, who gives generously to all without finding fault, and it will be given to you.

James 1:5 NIV

Who's Who

Going back to college and receiving my Bachelor's degree from the University of Denver was the best thing I could have done. My company paid my tuition, fees, and books for all four years. I did not know what a student loan was, thank goodness—Zero, out-of-pocket.

I applied myself and received all A's in the first year. When I got my first B, I cried like a baby. But I got over it by the time I got the second B. I received mostly A's all the way through. Writing papers was one of the things I enjoyed most. I could have made money writing papers for other students who disliked writing or were lazy.

Once, I had a paper due and was typing, like on a typewriter, and spent so much time watching my fingers hit the correct keys that I went too far down on the paper. For those of you who never used a typewriter, believe me, it has no idea about margins. When you think you have enough space left at the bottom of the paper for your margin, stop typing.

I went down to the bottom of the paper, leaving no margin, as I watched my fingers, trying to ensure I did not hit the wrong keys. I had to start the page over again.

This happened twice. Now I am frustrated. I began typing this page for the third time, but before I started, I drew a faint pencil line that could be easily erased to be my stopping point. When I saw the line, I knew to stop typing. It worked. In another chapter in this book, you will see an example of some of my typing skills from earlier in my childhood.

Being elected and serving as vice president of my class all four years was incredible. I learned critical leadership skills just by being the VP. These skills benefitted me and carried over into my work life. Don't forget that while attending classes and pursuing my degree, I managed a team of employees, traveled on my job weekly, and had a family. The school also granted me the prestigious honor of being selected and receiving the Who's Who Among Students In American Universities and Colleges award for those with a GPA of 3.2 or higher. Also, seniors are chosen based on leadership ability displayed in scholastic aptitude, community service, and extracurricular activities. Mom was so proud of me and the accomplishments I received when I graduated from the University of Denver.

My love for school probably began as far back as elementary school when teachers like Mrs. Johnson, our science teacher, Mrs. Stanley, our Auditorium teacher, and Ms. Dickey, our music teacher, showed us so much love and care that you couldn't help but be excited about school and learning. Ms. Dickey opened up her home to teach piano lessons to students, and my mom signed me up. For several years I went to lessons on Saturday mornings at her house.

I remember Mrs. Johnson teaching us about slavery, Black history, and about many of the struggles that were not in our textbooks, especially civil rights. She was the science teacher. Ms. Dickey taught us songs that later in my life I remember singing in church that never could be sung in schools now. We learned about opera and took field trips to see Broadway-quality plays. Mrs. Stanley taught us how to stand and deliver a memorized poem or a part you would do in a play, without being afraid to speak in front of a crowd and how to study and perform in plays. I would say that's equivalent to public speaking and acting taught at the elementary level. These skills helped me become who I am professionally and socially today.

There were special teachers in Junior High, too. Just a few, like Mrs. Council, Mrs. Derderian, and Mrs. Cooper, all cared enough to put their stamp on us. They taught us physical education, hygiene, nutrition, and how our eating affects our bodies. I wish them all well.

In high school, one lesson I know I keep passing on to my network of friends and family is one Mr. Jeffries taught us in Economics, and I quote, "I wouldn't co-sign a loan for my brother, sister, or their mother." He taught valuable lessons on managing and making your money work for you. So far, so good. We wouldn't want to leave out our favorite teacher, Mr. Glover. He taught History and Social Studies. He put a lot of drama and expression in his teaching, making learning enjoyable. I remember hearing him say, "Go west, young man, go west," as he dramatized it in motion. He was the teacher who knew his students well enough to look at them and shake his head.

One semester on the first day of class, Mr. Glover saw two friends and me walking into his classroom. He split us up immediately and said, as he pointed, "you over there (Gilda), you over there in the opposite direction (Marsha), and you over here (Me)." He knew us well enough to know we would talk in class. We were always together every semester. He would have to stop the lesson to tell us to stop talking during class. After he split us up, we just wrote notes and passed them back and forth.

At our ten-year class reunion, he was at the door of the hall, and when he saw Gilda, Marsha, and me, walk in the door together, he just shook his head with a smile from ear to ear and said, "I can't believe what I am seeing. You three are still together. I could not separate you; obviously, you have stood the test of time." He laughed and laughed. We all liked Mr. Glover. I would say he was one of a kind.

Miles in the Snow

I never had to take a school bus to school. From kindergarten through twelfth grade, I was a walker. I did not know anyone who took a school bus. Some kids took the public city bus in junior high and high school. There were no daycare centers or preschools then. In kindergarten, I walked one block to the Old McGraw School. After that, it was closed so a new one could be built.

From first grade through sixth grade, I attended Marr Elementary, which was about a three-and-a-half block walk. Junior high and high school were separate buildings on the same grounds as the elementary school. Also on those grounds were a recreation activity center, eight to ten tennis courts, five baseball diamonds, an ice skating rink, and many grassy areas to play on. The swimming pools were inside the junior high and the high school.

Television was new, and only a few people had one. The channels still needed to develop scrolling techniques and notifications. Newscasters did not make any weather-related announcements. You went to bed at night, and it was a certainty that you would go to school in the morning, as far as the weather was concerned. No snow was too much, and no temperature was too low for us to be unable to walk to school. I remember below-zero days and so much snow that you had to find a car track in the street to walk in.

School uniforms were not worn in my day. Boys wore slacks, and girls wore dresses, skirts, or jumpers. It was not permissible for girls to wear slacks. In the cold months, turtle-neck sweaters and shirts were typical. When the temperature dropped way down and the snowy days were standard, outerwear included: hats, scarfs, muffins, ear muffs, heavy coats, and boots. We wore snowsuits with waterproof coats and pants for the most frigid days. We walked to school in the morning, home for lunch and back, and then home after school ended. It did not matter how much snow was on the ground or falling from the sky or how cold it was, we made it, and there was no complaining.

We strolled along with our friends talking, occasionally picking up snow, and throwing snowballs at each other. When we came home for lunch, we ate and watched Soupy Sales, the host of a TV show for kids with funny side characters. He would announce what he was having the following day for lunch, and I would always ask to have the same thing, and usually, I did. It was a high point in my day, I then got bundled up once again, and back to school I walked.

Enduring these challenges toughened us up. Today's students, not so much. A two-hour delay will be called if the temperature is in the teens. If there are six or more inches of snow, you probably will get a day off. If the snow came early in the evening and the road crews had a chance to clear the streets, you may go to school in the morning. But, if it came overnight, look out, no school.

Snow Days, Really?

Public school students used to be tougher than they are today, especially in the northern states. Before global warming, winters seemed much harsher; the snow was measured and predicted usually in feet more often than inches. Today's students have it pretty easy, especially regarding weather-related school closings and lunch. I never had a snow day or delayed starts, nor was there any lunch at school.

At the elementary school where I worked in Pennsylvania, all students stayed at school for lunch, and no one went home anymore. Either the student brought theirs from home, bought it at the cafeteria, or received free lunch. In the winter, parents were expected to listen to the 11 PM news report and the 6 AM news update for the school closing/ delay report for the day. Scrolling across the bottom of the screen, in alphabetical order, the name of school districts within the viewing area could be seen throughout the newscast and subsequent programs. Parents had all eyes on this viewing, attempting to get advanced notice of what to expect in the morning. If it snowed in the evening, kids would go to bed hoping there was enough snow to close or delay school for them the next day. On the other hand, parents were praying that the amount of snow or cold would fall just outside the closing/delay limits. The district school superintendent miraculously turned into a meteorologist overnight, making the necessary call.

The number of inches of fallen snow could sometimes prevent school buses and walking students from makings it safely to school. Even the degree of cold could cause students to get frostbite and hinder their safe arrival at school. Pittsburgh is a very hilly city, making it more dangerous for walking students and busses.

If schools were closed for the day, teachers also would have the day off. If the call was to delay school, it was always a 2-hour delay for school buses and walkers. However, teachers have yet to get a two-hour delay. They have to brave whatever weather-related issue and get there at their regular time. "Not fair!" Working parents have to scramble to find someone to keep their child or children at a moment's notice when school is called off and to be with them and get them to their busses for the 2-hour delay. The district typically has two snow closure days built into the schedule. If more snow days were needed in a school year, those extra days were added to the year in June.

I have seen many children arrive at school unprepared for learning and unprepared for the weather they just braved. Some had on sneakers, no gloves or hats, and many had a coat or jacket that was not appropriate for the degree of weather. The required school uniforms were not very thick and didn't provide adequate warmth unless sweaters and extra items were bundled up in addition. Subsequently, there is sickness and loss of school days that maybe could have been prevented.

Our school had emergency dry clothes for kids to wear for the day. Theirs were washed, dried, and switched back at the end of the day. (Same process for kids who came out of uniform at any time) Parents should not only be on their A-game regarding the weather and how to best dress their children, but they also should have a very well-thought-out plan B for emergencies, especially weather events.

Frost Bite

As a student, I volunteered and participated in many things in school. I was in instrumental class, playing the violin, singing in the glee club, acting in plays, and many other things. When I went with the Girl Scouts to an autumn hay ride on a farm, I thought it would be fun. It started out that way. The afternoon temperature was cool when we arrived. They served us some hot apple cider and several baked goods. Someone talked to us about the farm and the animals. Soon we climbed in the back of a flat truck covered with hay or straw. We sat on the hay, and the horse-drawn trailer took off. It got darker and cooler as we went.

I could feel my legs and feet getting numb and cold. The horse couldn't have gone any slower. I kept thinking, hurry and let's get back to the barn, then to the bus, and home.

When we returned to the barn, I could hardly stand or walk. I could not wait to get home. When I arrived home, I explained to my mom how I felt and what was hurting. She immediately took me to the doctor and was told I had "frostbite." I did not know what that was, but it was painful. They told mom that I should stay in bed for several days.

When Monday came, I could not go to school because of the pain. There were things at school I did not want to miss, but I had too much pain. I was off for a week. Finally, my legs, feet, and body felt normal again. I never went hay riding again. I still have cold feet today, but I think that's because I have such a warm heart.

1967, The Year that Was

Wow, what a year 1967 was! Just listen to the ups, downs, excitement, and danger. Your senior year in high school is expected to be the most exciting. School clubs, senior trips, prom, graduation, and all that. It was all that.

Our basketball team was always hot. We went to state playoffs that year, beating everyone who dared meet us on the court. Our guys were awesome. Being on the Booster Club, the official school club that keeps the fans riled up in the stands, was like being an extra cheerleader. Everyone in the Booster Club wore unique shirts with school logos and held large pompoms in each hand. We understood the game's rules and knew when to quiet the stadium for our team's difficult shots and when to raise the roof during difficult shots on the opposing team, aiming to disrupt their concentration before their shot. We were good at what we did. Traveling with the team locally, regionally, and statewide was an exciting adventure to add to my senior year.

Our senior trip was long anticipated. Most of us had never traveled far, especially without our parents. A memo was sent to parents to see if any would like to be chaperones for the senior trip. My memo, as well as most others, has yet to make it home. Tell me, who wanted to go on their senior trip with one or both parents being chaperones? Come on now, really?

I didn't care where we were scheduled to go, just that we were going. Our trip was to Washington, D.C. We began turning in our deposit and payments for the trip at the beginning of the school year. I kept a register of the money paid and how much was left to be paid in my binder. Wow, almost time to start shopping for outfits. I did some babysitting and odd jobs to earn money for my trip. Mom always tried to dress me in the latest styles as best she could, and I was always clean and polished. On this trip, I planned to be FLY!

What? No, really? Is it true, it can't be? One month before the trip was scheduled to depart, we were advised that the trip had been canceled. No reason was initially given. Students snooped around until we heard that the teachers responsible for coordinating the trip were getting divorced, and no other teachers stepped up to take their place. The truth finally did get out, divorce. The teachers were getting a divorce. Couldn't they consider us and our needs and get the divorce later? After all, this is our senior year. We can't reschedule our senior year or our trip. Oh well, no senior trip. Bummer.

Prom was the next event to plan during my senior year. Almost all the girls were getting their gowns at Lerner's Dress Shop. They may have been different colors, but they would look nearly identical. I was determined to stand out. Ms. Gladys, our neighbor, was a seamstress, and I was aware of the beautiful outfits she made for herself and others. I asked mom if Ms. Gladys would make my prom dress. I did not want to look like all the other girls who bought theirs from Lerner's. Mom suggested I walk across the street and ask her myself. I did, and she said, "yes."

You must be wondering whether or not I even had a date for the prom. The answer is no. I haven't been asked. I had my eye on a guy who was not a fellow student. He was a slightly older family friend. Mom said he would definitely not be taking me to the prom. Ms. Gladys did make my dress, and it was beautiful.

Mom was instrumental in choosing my prom date. I recognized this after the fact. One Sunday, at church, a young man from a different high school, whom I was very familiar with asked, "Do you have a date for the prom?" Before I could say yes, which was a lie, mom said, "No." Adding that, "She would love to go with you." I was immediately appalled and angered. This was not the person I wanted to go anywhere with, much less prom. He was a nice guy from a good family, and his mother liked me. His mom thought I would one day be her daughter-in-law. We were in youth group together, and I knew he was boring, He was not at all talkative or funny, and most of all, he did not have the "look." You know what I mean. My date was not one of the cool kids. Anybody who our parents thought was right was definitely not.

Marsha, Gilda, and I decided to go as a group with our dates. We called around to decide where to go for dinner after the prom. Most of our classmates would go to Stanley Mania's, a favorite Chinese hotspot. We wanted to be different, not wanting to go where the crowd was going. We wanted something we could brag about. There were rumblings that Nancy Wilson, the jazz singer, would perform at the Elmwood Casino and Dinner Club in Windsor Ontario, Canada. They were known for entertainers like Sammy Davis, Jr., Johnny Mathis, Ray Charles, The Temptations, and many others of their caliber. After finding out how much everything would cost, I shared it with my group, including my date. It was decided that this was our place, and reservations were made. We were going "out of the country" for prom night dinner and entertainment. No one would top that.

When my date picked me up the night of the prom, he looked nice and had a corsage for me. I was ready and smiling on the outside but not very happy on the inside. How did I let this happen? He was not my knight in shining armor. All of this was going through my mind, but I was determined to make the most of it. How ungrateful. My friend and her date were picked up next. From there, we drove straight to the Latin Quarters, where the prom was held. Not one but two other couples joined us there as part of our group. The girls looked beautiful, and the guys cleaned up well too. We spent most of the time checking out what everybody wore and who they were with. I wanted everybody to see the dress Ms. Gladys had made for me. My date did not know anybody because he went to a different high school. I introduced him to a few people but could have done a better job. Other than a few dances, the rest of the prom was a blur. I just wanted to get to the Elmwood Casino and Dinner Club. Looking back, the way I acted was relatively shallow. I could have done better. I was not raised like that.

Four couples, including us, left the prom and headed to Canada. We crossed the border and through the U.S. Customs agents without a hitch. Only a couple of us were 18 years old. We all felt so grown up. There were no other prom couples around once we got there. None of us had been to a club before. We laughed and talked as we looked around and pointed out certain things we had never seen. Ordering our meal from a menu like this was a little uncomfortable. Our server was helpful and understood that this was a special night and our first time in a nightclub. Looking at the items on the menu, my date whispered that he did not have enough money for two dinners, we had to share. The server took our table's order. Our dinner was served in different stages. I liked that. It's been too long to remember what everyone ordered for their meal. However, I remember that my date and I enjoyed the shared entree.

The table has been cleared, and now it's time for the main attraction, the show. Every performer gave us a treat, and it was a time we were sure to remember for the rest of our lives. Most of the people in the audience were older than we were and probably wondered why we were here for such entertainers as these. After that night, Nancy Wilson became my idol. It made me feel like a grown-up being there. Everyone at the table really had a good time with dinner and the show. This was to be talked about for decades.

The dinner is finished, the show is over, and it's time to leave. How embarrassing it was to try to settle the bill with too little money. It could have been worked out before we arrived if I had known we were short. The other guys gave him the business about it. When it was time to go, we talked about what we wanted to do for the rest of the night. I knew I was ready to go home. My excuse was that my brother arrived from California today, and I needed to get home. It was a lame excuse, and half of it was true. We drove back through customs into the United States and home.

There was no discussion. I was taken home. When we got there, most of my family sat on the porch since it was quite a hot night. My brother Jack was telling of his escapades. My date walked me to the porch and said good night.

The best part of the night was showing off my dress, saying, "I went out of the country on prom night," and getting dropped off at home early. Looking back decades later, I feel bad that I acted so unseemly. I wish I had apologized. He has gone on to glory, and hopefully, one day, I will see him and apologize for my behavior and lack of compassion.

This year's events were not over yet. One month following my long-awaited and successful graduation and prom, one of my girlfriends and a couple of guys drove around and decided to walk on the beach at Point Pelee National Park in Leamington, Ontario, Canada. We had no problem going through customs even though my friend and I were not 18. (In 1967, where I lived, twenty-one was the legal age, and eighteen was the legal age later.) The guys were over 21. The U.S. agents asked, "are you U.S. citizens" and "did we have anything to declare," we answered "Yes" and "No," respectively. When we arrived at the park, we sat on the beach and talked while the guys attempted to catch some smelts (small fish similar to sardines).

When we returned to the U.S. and stopped at our favorite White Castle Hamburger Restaurant, we heard the news about the start of the infamous Detroit riots after an incident at the Algiers Motel where three young unarmed Black boys were gunned down. We watched and heard many emergency vehicles speeding along in all directions. Putting our radio on for updates, we soon understood the gravity of the situation and knew we needed to get home quickly. Many historical events are so vivid that you know exactly where you were when they happened: President Kennedy's Assassination, Challenger Space Shuttle Explosion, and the Detroit Riots, to name a few. I can say, "I was out of the country" when the riots started.

PART 11

Childhood

Since, then, you have been raised with Christ, set your hearts on things above, where Christ is, seated at the right hand of God. Set your mind on things above, not on earthly things.

Colossians 3:1-2 NIV

The Letter

When I was six years old, I typed and sent my grandma a letter in the mail. How could that happen since the computer had not been invented yet? Places like the Smithsonian and other museums have a device known as a "Typewriter." This device did not have memory, did not auto-correct, and there were no software, screens, monitors, or hard drives. It had no drives at all.

As a child, I remember multiple generations living together in the same dwelling. My grandparents lived with us too. This was the first time they lived in a home with indoor plumbing, a washing machine, and a bathtub. (The washer was a wringer type.) My grandmother was an at-home wife; after I was born, she cared for me when my mother went to work. We were close because, unlike babysitters, she did not leave at the end of the day. She lived there.

Several years passed after she moved to Michigan, and my grandmother wanted to see her sister. Arrangements were made to allow her to make a return visit to Mississippi. I will miss her because we were buddies. Skype, FaceTime, and cell phones had yet to be invented. Hand-written or typed letters were the way most people communicated.

You would always know when a letter came from home (down home), there was excitement as each person in the family read it. Everybody wanted to know how things and people were back home.

When we had watermelon, somebody always said, "It's just like a letter from home." I kept asking about grandma and saying how much I missed her; my mom suggested I send her a letter. I said, "OK." I did not know it, but there was a typewriter in the closet. This was my first time seeing or using one. I was excited. Did I mention that I was only six years old? This was before electric typewriters, ours was a manual.

Sitting at the typewriter, mom put paper in and rolled it to the spot where I was to begin typing. This was no word processor. She sat me right in front of it and positioned my tiny fingers on the metal keys. I was told to press each key, and that same letter would appear on the paper. Wow, this was fun. I pushed key after key, watching those letters appear on the paper. I liked this. I started going faster, and the letters would fly onto the paper. I had to remember to always hit the bar when I got to the end of the row so the paper would advance to the next row.

OK, you know I did not know all the names of the letters or how to spell any words, but I acted like I knew. When I was done, there were just random letters on the page, all of them spelling absolutely nothing. I talked as I typed, saying the word I assumed was showing up on the paper with each keystroke. "Dear Grandma, I miss you and hope you come home soon. Are you having fun? Tell everybody hello." When my letter was finished, and my pictures were drawn, mom helped me handwrite the envelope and put a stamp on it so it could be mailed. We went to the mailbox and dropped the letter in the slot. I was unsure how my grandma would get my letter out of that box.

Every day I would ask if she got my letter. It took forever before I learned she got it. It indeed was snail mail. Finally, she called and said she got my letter and that it was lovely to hear from me. She knew exactly what I had typed in the letter. She could read it. I knew she could.

Many years later, mom shared the letter with me and told me the story grandma told her. She and her sister sat on the porch as she opened the letter. When she began to read the letter, she could not stop laughing. Her sister kept asking over and over, "Emma, what is she saying?" Grandma could not stop laughing as her sister kept asking the same question. Eventually, she showed the letter to her sister, and the two of them laughed and laughed. I am sure it made their day and was a story to be told repeatedly.

She kept that letter all of her life. I was blessed to have mom give the original letter to me after grandma died. I still have it in my jewelry box on my dresser, and sometimes I take it out, read it, smile, and think about how much I loved my grandma, and she loved me. The letter is almost seventy years old and is in excellent condition. Look at the copy of the letter and envelope for yourself and feel the warmth inside as you smile. This is love.

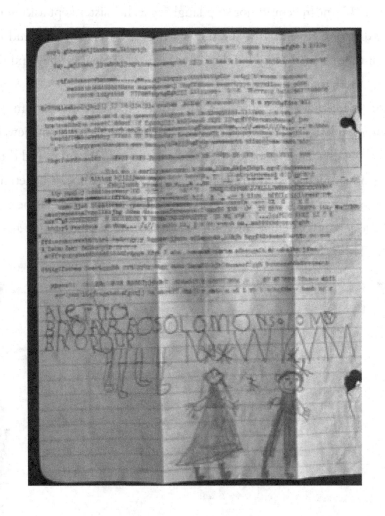

It's a Girl

I can't recall all the events that happened in my early life. Mom shared details with me about events that happened before I was five years old. An old saying states, "Truth is stranger than fiction..." as you might agree after reading further. Mom was an honest woman, and I know whatever stories she shared were true. This is "one for the books" and one of my favorites.

I snuck into the world at Herman Kiefer hospital one afternoon a long time ago. Everybody was excited about my arrival and gave me a warm welcome. Grandma's daughters only had boys, and it had been quite a few years since a baby came to live in the house. "It's a girl!" What a surprise. In those days, you did not have the technology to announce the gender of the child before that special day. You had to wait for the birth. Believe it or not, contrary to popular demand, I was a good baby: sleeping all night, not crying all the time, and allowing anyone to hold me. According to tales I have heard, I was a poor eater. You certainly couldn't tell that now. Not being a hearty eater was not an option in my family; we had the best cooks, and everybody enjoyed what was presented to them at mealtime. If the baby had a poor appetite, many home remedies and old wives' tales were used to get the baby to eat.

I had a small appetite and did not consume the amount of milk my mom thought I should. I would be rushed to the doctor far too often, for mom to hear, "Your baby is fine; she will eat when she is hungry," the doctor would say. After many visits, the doctor told mom, "Please keep this baby home until she is sick." I did not have any symptoms of being sick, but I didn't eat like they thought I should. Grandma made a concoction of evaporated milk, Karo syrup, and who knows what else they gave me to entice me to "drink up." The results were not to their liking. Grandpa took three buses to the outskirts of town to a place that sold goat's milk. They tried the goat's milk, then half and half, but no more than three or four ounces were consumed at any time for months.

When I was about two years old, I began to eat several small meals, more like snacks, throughout the day. I was healthy and full of energy but tiny.

Grandma kept me when my mom went to work. She would look at soap operas, and so did I, not knowing what they were about, just something to do. There were only about three or four channels. Young people today wouldn't be able to grasp that. There was no one to play with; all the boys who lived in the house were older and at school. The youngest among them was nine years older than me. Even if they were home, they would not have wanted to play with me; they never did.

Tied to a Tree

"Take your sister out in her stroller. It's a nice day", said mom. "I can't; my friends just came to get me to play baseball at the field," said Jack. "Take your sister for a ride before you go," said mom. When parents want a break, they send the kids outside to play. In my case, my brother Jack was eleven years older than I was. We did not have friends in common. I was only three years old. His friends would not have wanted to play baseball with me.

With his lips poked out and stomping his feet, we headed to the field, along with his friends, where the baseball diamonds were. I was happy to be out of the house. I saw some birds, a cat and lots of cars. The field was about three blocks from home and across a busy main street. After getting across the busy street, the park covered a large area. When we reached the location for his game, Jack tied me to a tree so I would not roll away while he played baseball.

Eventually, the nice air lulled me to sleep, and my brother Jack played until the game ended. By the time we got home, I was fully awake and well-rested. I enjoyed my outing.

Grandpa Kelly

This is the same ball field where Grandpa Kelly spent many of his days watching, talking to, and harassing many of those who were brave enough to engage him. This is where he advertised his products and found many customers. In a sense, he was always finding ways to be the provider for his family. He was, I would say, the first Entrepreneur in the family. Using the only skills he had, Grandpa Kelly always found inventive and sometimes not very legal ways to earn money.

With limited education, he found creative ways to support the family. He made and sold moonshine that he made in the basement. Even though he sold it at a slightly lower price than what it would cost in the store, he still made a profit. For those who only wanted a drink, he accommodated them also by selling shots. What a salesman he was. He served our local area, and neighboring states. Working this alone had to be quite challenging since he had never learned to drive. However, Grandpa Kelly found ways to transport his goods on the bus or train, and sometimes he could catch a ride. The products were packaged in a footlocker and cushioned with straw for protection from breaking while transporting them. He not only provided a product for profit, he was also what we called a loan shark. When anyone needed cash, he charged twenty-five cent interest on a dollar.

He told funny, inspiring stories but some were hard to believe. He always walked with a cane. It was more like a walking stick. It was not a purchased one, but one he found that was the right length. He whittled away enough of it to work as a cane. When he got in a heated discussion, you could see him hold that stick up and use it as an extended pointer finger as he ranted on and on to convince you of his point. Some old men on the ball field would engage with him until they were thoroughly exhausted. Then they all would laugh and turn to another subject. All the fellows waited anxiously for him to come to the ball field and engage with them daily.

The Ball Field

When he was at the family house, he would use that cane to tap on the floor, the porch, or anywhere to get the attention of anyone who could help him. From the porch, Grandpa Kelly would yell, "Hey" as he raised the stick high in the air to get the vendor's attention to stop the truck, especially the watermelon man. The truck would always stop and wait for him to get from the porch to the street to look at the produce and watermelons since he was slow. Looking back it is obvious now how much pain he was in when he walked. He always used that cane to get around.

Years later, everybody had fun telling stories about the past and laughing like crazy at ridiculous antics. We all laughed about some of my Grandpa Kelly's rants on the ball field. The spot where he sat was just a few feet from the tree where my brother tied me so he could play ball with his friends. I know that spot well. It was only then (in my thirties) that I heard this story about tying me to the tree for the first time. Jack, my brother, could not stop laughing as he told it. Popping up, I said, "what do you mean you tied me to a tree while you played baseball? You were crazy enough to tie me to a tree." Jack said, "I did not tie you to the tree. I tied the stroller to the tree." I was not laughing. "What if some bees or a dog tried to get me?" Laughing, Jack said, "they would have just got you, that's all." Even my mother started laughing, but believe me, she would not have been laughing that day if she only knew.

Puzzles

My family played many games together. I liked putting together jigsaw puzzles. The United States puzzle was fun. It was a great learning tool providing us with a way to learn about the states, capitals, and major industries or products for each one. Each piece was a different color. The name of its capital and pictures of important things the state provided was on the puzzle piece. When putting the puzzle together, we noticed how far each place was from where we lived. We talked about each state and questioned if we had any family members there. Some states seemed fun, and you automatically wanted to visit there; others were just pieces of the puzzle you needed to put in the right spot. Mom showed us the state she was born in; my aunt did the same.

Every day we watched the Mickie Mouse Club on television, and we knew that Disneyland was in California, and we all wanted to go there. I never went, nor do I have any interest in going now.

The New York piece was my favorite. I could remember many things about that state. We thought of the Macy's Thanksgiving Day Parade, New Year's Eve at Times Square with the ball drop, Broadway plays, and the Ed Sullivan show. His show came on every Sunday evening, and the entire family sat around the television to watch and enjoy it. There were more exciting things in New York than anywhere else. I could see the parade in my mind and imagine being there. That would be such a great experience. I planned to get there one day.

When I moved to New York, the thought of seeing the parade in person was still in my mind. The parade would have been on the top if I had a Bucket List. I went to the New York parade many times after moving there later in my life. Today, there are lots of cities with a Thanksgiving Day Parade, but Macy's parade is still the best parade ever.

Pay Bills

Before internet bill pay, people paid their bills in person or by snail mail, the U.S. Postal Service. Your statement would come in the mail, and the payment due date would give you about two to three weeks to get your payment back to them. You could purchase a money order or write a paper check to put in the mail to cover the amount you owe. When I was ten years old, my mom gave me a list of payments to make, the cash to pay each bill, and bus fare to get downtown and back. Accompanying my mom many times to know where each company was located and where to get off and on the bus gave me the courage to go and come without any doubt of completing this task successfully.

Walking from my house to the bus stop was simple. I would cut through the alley and see far down the street, knowing if the bus was coming before I got to the stop. If I saw it coming, my feet would take off running as fast as possible so I would not miss it and have to wait for the next one.

My first stop was the Electric Company, about three miles down the road. In Detroit, at that time, you could exchange burned-out light bulbs for the same wattage ones for free. Mom always gave me a bag of burned-out light bulbs to trade in for new ones. The point was not to break even one of them, or they would not make a free exchange. You exchanged like for like for free, assuming the bulb was not broken.

There usually was no line for exchanging the bulbs. Reading the wattage on each one and getting a new one with the same wattage was easy because I saw mom do it many times. She always allowed me to help. After changing the bulbs, getting in line to pay the bill was next. I took out the electric bill plus its money folded inside and paid the bill being careful to count the change I received. Leaving with the bag of new bulbs, I waited for the next bus and rode to the Telephone Company.

The Telephone Company was not far, less than a mile. I got off in front of the door and went in and saw a long line where I would pay the bill. When it was my turn, I had to reach up high to the counter to hand the bill and the money to the lady. Carefully, I counted any change I was due, never wanting to be short at the next stop. The Gas Company and the Water Company were only walking distance away; no bus this time. I repeated the payment process at each site and finally completed my assignment.

Sometimes mom would give me extra money to get a hot dog at the SS Kresge store. That was a real treat that did not happen often. After I ate my hot dog, I walked to the bus terminal and waited for the bus that would take me home. I was careful to look at the number and street name on the front of the bus because many buses came into the terminal. I could have easily gotten on the wrong bus if I had not been careful.

When I got home, mom and I would look at the bag of bulbs and each bill with its stamped date, time, and amount paid to ensure everything was done to her satisfaction. She would count her change, and she knew exactly how much she was supposed to get back down to the penny. Mom told me what a good job I had done and gave me a big hug. I loved it, and I felt very grown up at only ten years old.

My brothers were grown and gone. As my mom's only child at home, I was able to spend more time with her. At an early age, I learned things that required me to be responsible in transactions of money, shopping, and directions.

Learn from your parents; pay your bills as promised and always be on time. If you are late, it's a black mark on your credit record.

My job required me to be on the go from sun up to sun down and even late into the night at times. There was: work, mentoring matches, celebrations in the evenings, and some work on weekends. You ask, "how did that work for me?" It didn't always work well. This caused some things to be last minute.

Jackie

My brother Jack affectionately referred to as E. Jack in California, lived in the house before I started school. We were eleven years apart in age, so we did not have the same friends.

The most I remember about Jackie during the early years was his occasional coming home and leaving. Much of the memories were told to me by our mother. I already told you about the stroller ride. When I started kindergarten he left for the Air Force, and he never returned to the house to live. He visited on occasion during my school years, but we never had a close relationship during those years.

After I became an adult, I remember him coming home several times and some of the conversations we had over the years were quite humorous. Jack had a sense of humor that was not always noticeable until you got to know him and his essence. In fact, he could be funny beyond measure.

Jack also had a very serious side. He loved reading the newspaper and the bible and retained so much that he could quote it one, two, three. He was a consumer of knowledge and was self-taught in many venues. He read the newspaper end to end, the bible cover to cover, and any other thing he got his hands on. He was pretty smart. I went to church every week, and he went with me, also.

When Jack lived in California, he worked as a taxi driver in San Francisco for many years. He knew the city like the back of his hand. This was something he really liked doing, probably because with his gift of gab he could engage his riders from the time they got in the cab to the time they got out. It was kind of like being a celebrity, and he was on stage. The passenger was a captive audience. Jasmine remembers doing a ride-along with him while he drove.

Jack was a fan of Jazz, Public Radio, and learning. He was well-read on almost anything, and I remember him being very intelligent and up-to-date on many topics, being self-taught. The newspaper would stay so long it would be turning yellow waiting for him to finish it (smile). Jairo said he could also listen to several tracks on the Jazz station and at the end could easily rattle off who was on the trumpet, drum, keyboard, and other instruments. I do remember hearing lots of music from his room when I was young. He even tried playing an instrument but unfortunately did not continue that.

When he visited me in Pittsburgh, he asked if I would stop and pick up a Sunday paper for him. He went through section by section, marker or pen in hand, every word was consumed. I don't know what he searched the paper for the most, the race track or the news. A couple of days passed and one morning on my way out to work, I gathered the papers up and took out to the trash. Just wanted to straighten up the living room a bit. After I was gone, he got up, made coffee, and looked for the remnants of the paper, and couldn't find any. He called me to ask where the paper was, and I told him I took it out. He was livid, but not mean, saying, "what did you do that for I am still going through it?" I learned my lesson for the remaining time that he was with me, I never took the paper out, I left that chore up to him.

I was always the "little girl" until I got married and had a child of my own. My daughter Tai Tanisha and his daughter Jasmine are only two weeks apart in age, unfortunately, we were in New York, and they were in California, so the girls never got to play with each other as children. They did meet once, but I do not think either of them remembers that. They were probably only five or six. We have made up a lot of that ground since then.

When Jack passed away, we all went to celebrate his life and had the most wonderful time with his four children and friends. We tried to talk and remember stories and events to share that the other ones did not know. Under the circumstances, we had a good time together. Rest in peace, Jack.

Make the Bed

There is a certain way to make a bed, and I adhere to that standard to this day. As a child, we knew that after they were washed and hung on the line outside to dry, sheets had to be dampened and ironed before being put on the bed. There could not be any wrinkles in the sheets or pillowcases when you made the bed.

The fabric used for making sheets was cotton in those days, guaranteeing wrinkles when washed. Before we had clothes dryers, weather permitting, everything that was washed would be line-dried, usually outside. Now, most sheets are made of artificial fabrics, and most, if not all, are wrinkle-free.

Putting fresh sheets on the bed that had been hanging out in the sun smelled great. It made for a good sound sleep. It traumatizes me to have my sheet come undone during the night. There is a way to tuck the corners that would not allow this to happen. My bed is always perfect. Each morning I make my bed before getting ready for the day. It has to be perfect when I make it, or I won't be able to sleep in it.

Occasionally, a grandson or granddaughter would help me make the bed, and they would complain when I asked them to re-do a part, and all I could hear was fussing. They laugh and tell each other, "you don't want to help grandma make her bed." I will get out of bed to adjust something before I can go to sleep.

Remember, Carlos, says my bed is my "best friend." It just has to be perfect. When talking to him on the phone, he sometimes asks me how my "best friend" is doing. We both know what he is talking about.

Not Just the Library

The neighborhood kids walked everywhere. When we were about ten years old, Carolyn, Calvin, and I would go to the library which was close to a mile away. We spent lots of time looking through the card catalog to find books we thought were interesting so we could check them out. Just across the street from the library was a funeral home. We knew that dead people were there. I don't remember whose bright idea it was to go in and look around, but we did. We would be very quiet, and there was no laughing. If they were dead, they could not have heard us anyway.

We went from room to room, looking at each name, their age, and what they wore. We tried to think about the kind of person they could have been. Did they have kids like us or if they were old like our parents and grandparents? How did they die? Why did they die? Each week we would stop in and look at the people laid out for viewing and put our names in the book near them, to say that we stopped by.

One day we went to the library and had to hurry home because our family was going somewhere, and we did not have time to go to the funeral home. We can stop at the funeral home next week and spend extra time there.

This week we planned to stop at the funeral home on the way to the library and spend a little extra time. We did not get to go there the previous week. We did a tour of the viewing room and signed our names in the visitor books. Something was different this time. We saw a baby that was dead. It was in a box like a shoe box. We were so sad. We couldn't stop looking at that baby because it looked like a doll. Finally, we left, went to the library, got our books, and went home. We wanted to ask why the baby was dead, but we did not say anything. We stopped going to the funeral home after that. It was too sad after seeing that cute baby.

Streetlights

Children always like to be competitive. Sometimes before school, we needed to get bread or something from the store to make our lunch, and our parents would send us to pick it up. "Hurry back so you can get to school and not be late," mom would say. If you saw another child on your block when you went to the store, you would try to say before they did "first-all-day." If you got it out first, they would say, "second-all-day." When you saw other kids from your block after the trip to the store, they would be told that someone had already picked first and second all day. They were left with third-all-day, and so forth. Each day brought a new "pecking order."

There would be hopscotch, baseball, jump rope, and hide-n-go-seek after school. Sometimes we rode bikes and other games. First-all-day meant something. You could pick teams and anything else we played, first. We played and rode our bikes until almost dark. Of course, this was after chores and homework.

When the street lights were getting ready to come on, they would illuminate gradually. They took about two minutes to get fully bright. We all knew because our parents probably got together and agreed that when the street lights came on, you had to be on the porch. Since they came on slowly, you could finish a turn, run as fast as possible, and get to your porch before the light was fully on. None of the parents had to come looking for us or call us. We knew the drill. We all made it every day.

PART 12

Generational House

For God so loved the world that he gave his one and only Son, that whoever believes in him shall not perish but have eternal life. For God did not send his Son into the world to condemn the world, but to save the world through him.

John 3:16-17

Women of the Family

How many people can you fit in a house listed as a three-bedroom, one-bath house? Let me count the ways. Let's see.

When the industrial revolution began, many African American individuals and families migrated from southern to northern states for better economic opportunities. My grandmother, Emma, and grandfather, Kelly, did, also. In doing so, some traditions were kept and enriched the family, but as time and technology moved forward, it became inevitable for some things to change. Four of their children also moved north and started their families and new lives. In fact, their children came north to prepare a place for the family before Emma and Kelly did. It has always been a tight-knit family, and living together was sometimes challenging but love always won out.

The three sisters, Lillie, Bea, and Emma, found work, saved, and were able to be the first in the family's history to purchase a home in 1943. In the United States, a woman could not sign and buy a house on her own then. A man had to do the purchasing. Ok, don't let me get distracted and on a rant about that. Back to the facts, just the facts. A cousin, Samuel White, who grew up with them in Mississippi, lived and worked in the city of Detroit. He agreed to purchase the home for them and then transfer the ownership into their names. That's precisely what happened.

Our family became property owners for the first time, which would not have been possible in the south. They had a spirit of generosity for giving, helping, and sharing to make others' lives better as well.

Grandma Emma and Grandpa Kelly were in one bedroom. Aunt Bea and Uncle Lee in another. Mom and I were in the third one. Hold on, and there were nine more people there. Two rooms that needed to be better insulated were attached to the back of the house. One above the other, behind the kitchen on the lower level, and behind the bathroom on the upper level. Those back rooms were pretty cold in the winter and quite warm in the summer. Melvin and James slept in the one behind the kitchen, and Robert and Jack in the one behind the bathroom. Accessing Robert and Jack's room, whether coming in or going out of the room, required passing through the bathroom. Suppose someone was using the bathroom in any manner; too bad. Aunt Emma and her two daughters slept on the pull-out bed in the dining room. If that wasn't enough, the family had roomers in the basement bedroom. There was only one full bathroom upstairs and a toilet in the basement. With that many people in one house, I never knew of any congestion waiting in the hallway for the bathroom or trying to get ready for school.

Nurturing is what my family has always been good at. Gatherings, centered around meals throughout the year, especially on holidays, were always happening. Out-of-town family members came, and I was glad to see them come and equally pleased to see some of them go. It was a time when we stayed up late, laughing and giggling until we all fell asleep.

Grandma always spent time cooking and giving directions to everyone around her. It wasn't harsh or mean, just direct. Everyone followed her orders without a challenge. Meals were scrump-deli-ishous. Everything imaginable was prepared perfectly without a cookbook. My grandmother knew her way around a kitchen. Mom was equally as good in my mind or better. There was nothing my mom couldn't make. Indeed she spent countless hours helping her mom and learning everything she could. There was no television or other electronic stuff to fill your time as a child when my mom and her sisters were growing up. You learned the basics of cooking and cleaning. Chores were what you did, especially when you were raised on a farm, as they were.

The women of the family: my grandmother, mom, and two aunts Bea and Emma, worked together like a hand and a glove. One aunt wasn't as handy but was good at following instructions. It was rhythm in motion. All of the dishes came together at precisely the same time as planned. Being in the kitchen with the ladies made me feel grown up. I was young and didn't realize what I was experiencing, but now I can appreciate the bond they shared as they cooked together. As my mom's "pride-n-joy," I stuck to her like glue. I wasn't made to, but I always chose to be at her side. We shopped, prepared, and served most meals together. I liked watching her and desired to emulate her in every way.

I was focused and wanted to please the women. Love permeated the process and the taste. The family always ate meals together. That's not the norm today. I can't recall when we didn't have supper together until the boys were teens and got into sports. We talked, laughed, and ate until we were full.

It wasn't only cooking I remember learning from the ladies in my family, but how to fold a fitted sheet with precision and no wrinkles. Even today, some friends ask how I can fold a fitted sheet as I do. Some cousins and my grandchildren refuse to learn the "fitted sheet" lesson. They give up too quickly. I give all the credit to the nurture my mom shared with me.

My daughter can cut a chicken, make anything in the kitchen, and is a beast at folding fitted sheets. She is the fourth generation that's keeping these traditions. Now when you are talking about her kids, that's a "horse" of a different "color." Her sons picked up her love of cooking, but not so much for keeping things tidy. However, her daughter can win the award for keeping things tidy, while she and her husband are experimenting with new cooking techniques in many areas. I expect her to surpass her brothers in this area at some point. We will see.

My Aunt Bea and Uncle Lee were the only drivers in the family. Mom did not always have to go to the market; some foods were brought to you by men on trucks driving through the neighborhood, calling out their products. Thank goodness for the delivery men. Grandpa Kelly showed me how to thump a watermelon on the back of the truck to see if it was ready. It worked every time for him, but it still does not work a hundred percent of the time for me. Grandpa had that magic touch. The watermelon, spice, vegetable, ice, and insurance men were regulars coming through the neighborhood.

Whoever was cooking that day prepared enough food to fill everybody with some leftovers; none of us knew hunger. The one black and white small screen television worked, and everyone enjoyed whatever was on. There was no bickering over the remote to change the channel to watch what you wanted to see because there was no remote (smile). You had to get up and walk to the television to change the channel, and there were only three or four stations.

Our dining room table doubled as a makeshift piano. I liked saying I was taking piano lessons but did not like attending classes. Practice at home after school wasn't so bad. We did not have a piano to practice on. I practiced on a cardboard image of the eighty-eight keys that went along the edge of the dining room table. No one knew for sure if I was practicing or striking the correct keys because the cardboard did not make a sound. When I said, "I'm finished practicing," mom said, "ok." I just wanted to finish and get outside.

My fingers would get a wack or two by my teacher when I would misplay a note. My poor fingers, I am surprised they work at all now. When Stevie Wonder made the song Fingertips (Part 1), he must have gotten his fingers whacked from time to time when he misplayed a note, too. I would love to talk to him about his "fingertips."

Aunt Bea was a gardener. She kept the yard beautiful with plants and shrubs. The backyard garden had edible plants like rhubarb, strawberries, greens, tomatoes, scallions, lettuce, squash, strawberries, grapes, and other items. She nurtured the most beautiful roses and a magnificent Snowball Tree. The women were all fantastic cooks and kept our bellies full of healthy savory foods and baked treats. They were good enough to say they were "slap your mama good."

Serious cooks and bakers were all over this family. My grandma was the main cook (now called the Head Chef) in a restaurant down south before coming north. She could "burn." Mom was also the head cook at the soup kitchen at church, where many who needed help and those who were homeless could get food. For many years, she put her cooking skills to work in the middle school cafeteria.

Everything was handmade with fresh ingredients. The farmers market provided bushels of produce, which they canned and put away in the basement "fruit cellar." Later, the canned goods were pulled out as needed in the winter months. They prepared fruits, vegetables, jellies, and wine. I began to be included in these processes at a reasonably young age and can still do most of what I learned today.

Most of the canning activities happened on the stove that was in the basement. My mom made homemade lye soap in the basement from old cooking oil, to use for laundry, dishes, and bathing. It was a way to save a buck and use items we would now throw away. "Waste not want not" was their motto. I believe that is how the money stretched as far as it did. One thing that was not in the basement was a clothes dryer. That's unless you call the rope clothesline and wooden clothespins a dryer.

In the winter, you hung clothes in the basement next to the coal furnace; in the summer, clothes were hung outside on the line. When the clothes were dry, the ironing began. I did not like that job. You moistened the clothes, rolled them up, and placed them in a plastic bag in the refrigerator so they would not dry out until you finished ironing them. That would include sheets, pillowcases, underclothes, and outer clothes. Glad those days are over. I don't plan to iron any more underwear in my lifetime. If I could have paid someone to do my ironing chores, I would have gladly done so. Come to think of it, why did we hang the clothes out to dry, only to bring them in, moisten them, and shove them in a plastic bag in the refrigerator? The funny thing is, today, I have an iron, for what I don't know, but I do not have an ironing board. When I am quilting, I do use the iron to press seams but not for ironing clothes. I was scarred from all that ironing, especially the underwear.

The smell of fresh rolls and bread could make you gain ten pounds just smelling it. I liked to help by watching when the dough would rise so I could punch it down. Everyone was attracted to the kitchen because of the smell alone. The fresh rolls could barely stick around until mealtime. Neighbors even found their way to our home when the rolls were made. There could have been a sign on the front porch saying, "hot fresh rolls ready now." Our favorite treats were homemade baked rolls and mom's ice cream.

Growing up then versus now was different. I learned and experienced many things that will get you through when the chips are down, even today. I was taught how to make something literally out of nothing which would taste good. Everything homemade was better than store-bought and made with love—there is nothing like those hand-me-down recipes from that bygone era. I have most of mom's handwritten recipes in my cabinet.

Whatever gifts each family member had were lovingly and eagerly shared with others. We didn't purchase clothes for special occasions; one aunt made them all. We didn't go to the hairdresser; one aunt was a beautician. We didn't have to catch rides with friends and neighbors; one aunt drove us everywhere. We didn't have to read a cookbook; all the ladies taught us how to cook. From making lye soap, and homemade root beer, to cooking, canning, sewing, curtain stretching, gardening, hairdressing, baking, laundry, and much more. You could become an expert at almost anything if you applied yourself. Everyone was patient and compassionate in their giving of themselves.

I began this book with the feeling that our family hand me downs, were life lessons, nurturing, and those wonderful handwritten recipes. Now I know that the "hand me down" was LOVE.

My grandmother, mother, and aunts were nurturers, and that gene has undoubtedly passed through to me, my daughter Tai-Tanisha, and many others in the family. They were wise, resourceful, and passed along invaluable skills while lending a helping hand in the process. Prayer and faith in God were always a component of our family. Without it, I could not imagine how we made it. We were never lacking and always seems to have enough to share. There is no way to know what financial category we fell in as a family, but I don't believe we were middle class. Ask anyone of us, and we will tell you we definitely were not poor.

The narration of events in this memoir has rekindled joy and has put a smile on my face in the writing. As I wrote the memories it brought tears to my eyes and a feeling of a warm hug. I desire to share this picture of love with my family, friends, and others to enjoy. For some of you, it will be a glimpse of days gone by that can not and will not be able to return. Others of you will want to scratch your head and ask, "is that how they did that back then?" The phrase "those were the good old days' surely applies here.

All families should reflect on the good times and leave memories for future generations to savor. Some families have lost the sheer bond of multiple generations sharing, living, loving, and celebrating special celebratory moments, primarily due to distance. I firmly believe that the glue that holds and unites families is strong and is sometimes ready to make memories happen again. Now is the time. It only takes one to get the ball rolling. Will you be the family member to reach out?

Epilogue

$\mathcal{D}$o you ever wonder how you got here? I mean, where you are in life? I did. It led me to write this book and discover how my personality and life have evolved to where I am today. After reading these stories, you should see that my life has been bringing me to this point all along. Funny how Destiny seldom walks down the same road as you. Looking back, what I hold in my heart (my box) is the most important thing.

Too many times, I heard the phrase, "Great things come in small packages." If I were a box, a very small one, inside would be amazing things. So much is in my box that one might imagine that it would take a huge box to hold it all. A sign on the outside states, "DO NOT TOUCH." Most items are so valuable that they can not be touched, and many can not be seen with the naked eye. Security is a high priority.

Just thinking about them, I immediately get a warm, fuzzy, ominous feeling as I consider each item. I never want to forget any of the things inside. Let me begin by telling you about a few of the items. Without a doubt, one of the most essential things inside is my childhood memories: my mother and father, the neighborhood, church, school, and friends. Memories of my daughter's birth and growing up years are in the box. Especially the time she was left sitting on the sidewalk in Brooklyn because she wanted to have a tantrum about a bubble gum machine.

Many photographs line the box and bring chuckles, smiles, tears, and occasionally shivers as I hold them. My mom saved my elementary school report cards and passed them to me; they are in the box. The memories that surface about my friends, teachers, and classes are unforgettable when I think about them. I even remember one of the songs we sang in the Glee Club, "Bless This House Oh Lord We Pray, Keep It Safe By Night And Day." I love that song. I have caught myself humming it at times. Based on the title and words, I am sure kids are not singing that in schools today. They expelled God years ago.

In the box are many of my mom's hand-me-down, handwritten recipes, yum. Oh yes, Aunt Bea's Blueberry Cobbler recipe is in there too. The memory of helping make homemade ice cream. That memory will always be in the box.

When I graduated from the University of Denver, some of my family traveled to support me. They wanted to surprise me, and that memory will never leave the box. After the ceremony, my mom said, "I am so proud of you and Jack, too." "What? Jack? He is not even here. My older brother Jack wasn't able to make it to the ceremony. The memory of graduation will always live in the box.

Many friends span the country, especially those I call my *Sisterhood*. I connected with most of them mainly through my travels with work, and those friendships will never leave the box. These are people who far exceed the title of friend. We all are close and communicate with each other frequently. I can think of special memories with each of them in the box. These friends are what you would call "Soul Mates." We encourage each other, pray for each other, cry with each other, and, most importantly, we celebrate and laugh with each other. It's like we know each other inside and out and occasionally know each other's thoughts. Each brings a different gift to the table to share. Above all else, one gift we all share is the Lord Jesus Christ.

Marsha's daughter and grandkids consider us both their grandmas. I feel blessed because of them in my life. We have known each other since first grade. When we talk on the phone, we laugh and cut up. This is something money can not buy. Too precious. (We have been friends for more than sixty years.) Oh no, I told you my age.

I hope I can trust you with the most valuable thing in my box, the Fruit of The Spirit: Love, Joy, Peace, Patience, Goodness, Kindness, Gentleness, Faithfulness, and Self Control. The most valuable thing in the whole world, much less my box, is Love. Because with Love, all the other things are possible. The lessons God taught me are in the box. The gifts He has given me are in the box. The health He has blessed me with is in the box. Praise God.

Sometimes we find challenges in our life. But God has taught me how to learn from my brokenness. My testimony positions me to be a blessing to others in their challenges and brokenness. He promised never to leave me or forsake me, and that GOD alone, "will redeem it all." Never forget the power of Worship. Not every battle is won with the sword.

Every good thing comes from above, and they are in the box. I retrieve them as needed, enjoy them as needed, think about them as needed and share them as needed. My box is small but amazingly valuable, and I can not live without it. It doesn't belong in a vault or safe deposit box to protect its valuables because I access it often and need it close at hand. I know God watches over it and me constantly, so I know it will always be with me.

"HOWEVER, NOTHING BEFORE ITS TIME"

"THIS IS MY STORY, AND I AM STICKING TO IT"

My Bucket List - Paris

This has been and still is the most incredible life one could imagine: the people, the places, the children, the jobs, and the Love of God. I am so very grateful for the life I am living, everything is not perfect, but I couldn't be happier. There is joy every day. I wake up wondering what I can learn today and what I can share.

Hopefully, there are more memories to create and pass on, but in closing, here are a few of my next steps. I refer to them as my Bucket List.

The French language and dialect, one of the romance languages, has always sounded so dreamy. As far back as I can remember, Paris has held a calling card for me. When the term "Bucket List" became widely used instead of your "Wish List," I immediately added Paris to mine. I don't know anyone in my inner circle who has been there, other than my niece Jasmine, but more often than not, I have heard of certain must-see attractions. The world seems much more intimate since commercial air travel became available to far-off places like Paris.

In college, I took enough painting and art classes as electives that I was almost awarded a minor in art. Still trying to figure out where my love of art came from, but I became hooked. Even my love of quilting falls under my love of art. Why were so many world-renowned painters from France and the neighboring countries? I don't know. The

Impressionist period (1832-1883) is one of my favorites, with artists like Monet, Renoir, Van Gogh, Degas, Cezanne, and Matisse.

The most exciting things I plan to experience are French pastries, crepes, architecture, and the many museums. My first stop will be at various museums. I don't intend to leave without seeing all I have longed to see. At the top of my list are the following:

- The Louvre - with 35,000 masterpieces on display
- The Musee d'Orsay - houses the most extensive collection of Impressionist and Post-Impressionist works
- The Palais Garnier Opera House - setting for the original Phantom of the Opera
- Pont Alexandre III & Grand Palais - known for large artworks
- Palace of Versailles - castle of the last monarch, King Louis XIV & Queen Marie Antoinette

After I have stood in enough long lines, I want to eat at some notable restaurants specializing in fine French Cuisine before stopping at the Eiffel Tower and cruising down the Seine River. Next, I will take in a show at the Moulin Rouge and stroll through the pricy shops on the Champs-Elysées (the Times Square of Paris).

Finally, I will ascend to Montmartre & The Sacre Coeur Basilica, the highest point in Paris, and take amazing pictures to share with everyone on my return home. That is, assuming I come back or choose to make that my new home. After all, it is the city of "love." How do they say it, "I may be old, but I'm not dead." This trip alone will make a fantastic memoir, you will see. Until next time, happy memories.

"In the same way, let your light shine before others, that they may see your good deeds and glorify your Father in heaven.

Matthew 5:16 NIV

Appendix A

ABOUT THE AUTHOR

$\mathcal{B}$orn in Detroit, Aletha Joyce Solomon is a retired Avaya Communications manager. She graduated from Northwestern High, and Parker Institute in Detroit, the University of Denver, and the Harty Bible School, in Pittsburgh. Her first published work was *From the Rising of The Sun,* which documents her genealogy and family history, encouraging her to continue writing. Her past times include matching Christian mentors with children, quilting, working with Angel Tree prison ministry, assisting the community with free tax preparation, and advocating in many areas for seniors. She has a deep love for children and family. God has placed a magnificent *Sisterhood* in her life to be encouragers to each other. She is a member of the Colorado Community Church and part of a small group there. First and foremost, she is a child of the King and is fully committed to the Gospel of Jesus Christ.

Acknowledgements

Thanks to my incredible family: my daughter Tai-Tanisha and her husband (Ret.) MSG Michael Lawrence Simmons; my grandchildren Rafael Roberto Tejada and his wife Raelyn Tejada; Carlos Roberto Tejada; Michelle Tanisha Maxwell and her husband Akeem Maxwell; Lieutenant Michael Lawrence Simmons II; and Kristia Faith Blow. My great-grandchildren Ava'Marie Elizabeth Tejada; Gaven Parker-Brown; Sky Darnae Campbell; and Ka'Rina Lily Tejada, all of whom I dearly love.

I want to thank all who encouraged me on this journey and pushed me to finish my work so all can enjoy it. Thanks to my super Beta Readers: Rev. Eddie Morales; Rowland McCoy, DDS; Marsha Webb; Kathleen Grehl; Chaplin (Ret.) Alex Brown; Delores Rice Brown; Derek-Jan Love; Sandra Banks; Laurine Teeuwissen; and Tai-Tanisha. Your time and feedback have made this book all that it can be.

I could not have done this without my unique sisterhood that resides across many states. At all times, we are only a phone call away and are ready to celebrate the highs and pray for the lows in each other's lives. I pray God's blessings and favor follow you all your days. Thank God for: Marsha Webb; Rev. Sheila Johnson; Leonora McCormack; Tai-Tanisha; Silby Long; Emily Findlay, Ph.D.; Bobbette Thompson;

Michelle Bolton; Ida Meadows; Lois Tyler; Gwendolyn Couts; Iris Kyles; Margaret Richard. My love for each of you is undying.

Special shout-outs to others who encouraged me; may God's blessing be upon you: Mary Carr; Valerie Metzler; Roberta Floyd; Melvin & Shirley Ann Metzler; Annie Grace Anglin; Kathleen Grehl; Estella Patterson; Delores Rice Brown; Pastor Robert Russell; Delphia Macon; Latoi Williams; Vicki Anderson-Redwood; Joanne Galinowski; Arlene Claughton; Viola Craddock; Denese Exum; Shontel Reed; Winnie Utley; Ernestine (Violet) Harris-Dungee; Judy Ballard; Lillian Woodham; Sue Hunt; Phyllis Dye-Rhodes; Z.I Fleming, Jr; Jeffery Griffin: and Libya Wilson-Moore.

Thanks for the prayers and fellowship of those who walk with me in ministry: Vicki Bryant; Gillian Ngola; Becky O'Guin; Kay Kiser; Valerie Bellamy; Rev. Sheila Johnson; Denise, and Curt Miller.

Thanks to my editor: Jasmine Peterhans, my favorite niece. I am truly grateful for your knowledge and assistance in this work. The fortitude and strong-willed push I needed to complete all aspects were welcomed even when I did a bit of whining. You could not see the petulant tossing of my head as I reluctantly agreed. On this journey, I realized that you are so much like me that we could only laugh at each other at times. These words will forever be in my heart, and I will think of you when I hear them. (Loquacious, non sequitur, and persnickety) You and I alone know what this means, I hope it perpetually brings smiles to your face when you hear or think of these words (smile). May God bless you and everything you put your hands on. Writing this book and working with you has grown me in the effort as I shared buried nuggets about our family. You know all we went through. Thanks for being my favorite niece (my only niece); I love you.

This is a special message for my new great-grandchild who will arrive not long after this book is published. I can't wait for you to get here. I don't even know your name. When you arrive you will recognize me, I will be the one smiling ear to ear. Rafael and Raelyn are excited to add you to our loving family. We love you already. We are all waiting to meet you. Soon you will be on your way. God bless your journey.

In loving memory of my mother, Lillie Solomon, my father, Othello, Aunt Beatrice Harris, Aunt Emma Metzler, Uncle Willie (Buster) McCoy, my grandparents Emma McCoy and Kelly McCoy, and others who are no longer with us.

Thanks to my publishing consultant Eve Ardell and the team at Author House Publishing.

God bless each of you and provide all of your needs. Thank you Jesus, for the spirit of love, joy, fellowship, and laughter.

Printed in the United States
by Baker & Taylor Publisher Services